EDMONDS

BEST of BAKING

EDMONDS

BEST *of* BAKING

hachette
NEW ZEALAND

ISBN: 978-1-86971-341-6

Published in 2010 by Hachette Livre New Zealand Ltd

This edition published in 2016 by Hachette New Zealand Ltd
Level 2, 23 O'Connell Street, Auckland, New Zealand

The chapters in this book were originally published as four separate volumes in 1999.

Text and photography © Goodman Fielder New Zealand Ltd 2010
EDMONDS and SURE TO RISE are trademarks of Goodman Fielder New Zealand Ltd
The moral rights of the author have been asserted

Cataloguing-in-Publication data is available from the National Library of New Zealand

Cover and internal design by Seymour Designs and Hachette New Zealand Ltd
Printed by 1010 Printing, China

CONTENTS

INTRODUCTION

Welcome to *Edmonds Best of Baking*. Since 1907 Edmonds has helped many New Zealand cooks produce wonderful, tasty treats for family and friends.

The recipes in this book expand on the fine baking sections provided by the original *Edmonds Cookery Book*. *Best of Baking* contains both traditional Edmonds favourites as well as contemporary recipes.

From all the Edmonds team, we wish you many hours of great baking!

BISCUITS
and SLICES

AFGHANS

200 g butter, softened
½ cup sugar
1¼ cups Edmonds standard flour
¼ cup cocoa
2 cups cornflakes

CHOCOLATE ICING
2 cups icing sugar
2 tablespoons cocoa
¼ teaspoon butter
¼ teaspoon vanilla essence
2 tablespoons boiling water, approx.

walnuts (optional)

Cream butter and sugar until light and fluffy. Sift flour and cocoa. Stir into creamed mixture. Fold in cornflakes. Spoon mounds of mixture onto a greased oven tray, gently pressing the mixture together. Bake at 180°C for 15 minutes or until set. When cold ice with Chocolate Icing. To make the Chocolate Icing, sift icing sugar and cocoa into a bowl. Add butter and essence. Add sufficient boiling water to mix to a spreadable consistency. Decorate with a walnut if desired.
Makes 30.

AFGHAN SLICE

Press afghan mixture into a 20 x 30 cm sponge-roll tin. Bake at 180°C for 25 minutes or until set. When cold, ice with Chocolate Icing.

ALBERT SQUARES

125 g butter

¾ cup sugar

2 eggs

2 teaspoons golden syrup

½ teaspoon vanilla essence

1 cup currants

2 cups Edmonds standard flour

2 teaspoons Edmonds baking powder

pinch of salt

½ cup milk

ICING

1½ cups icing sugar

½ teaspoon vanilla essence

water to mix

3 tablespoons coconut

finely grated lemon zest (optional)

Cream butter and sugar until light and fluffy. Add eggs one at a time, beating well after each addition. Beat in syrup and vanilla. Fold in currants. Sift flour, baking powder and salt together. Fold sifted ingredients into creamed mixture alternately with milk. Spread into a greased 20 x 30 cm sponge-roll tin that has been lined with baking paper on the base. Bake at 180°C for 30 minutes or until centre springs back when lightly touched. When cold, ice and cut into squares. To make the icing, mix icing sugar, vanilla and sufficient water to make to a spreadable consistency. Ice and sprinkle with coconut and lemon zest.

ALMOND BISCUITS

125 g butter, softened
½ cup sugar
1 egg
½ teaspoon almond
essence

1½ cups Edmonds standard flour
1 teaspoon Edmonds
baking powder
12 to 15 blanched almonds

Cream butter and sugar until light and fluffy. Add egg and almond essence, beating well. Sift in flour and baking powder. Mix to a firm dough. Roll pieces into balls. Place on a greased oven tray and press lightly with the palm of your hand. Press half a blanched almond on each. Bake at 180°C for 15 minutes or until cooked. Makes 25.

ALMOND CRESCENT BISCUITS

200 g butter, softened
½ cup caster sugar
½ teaspoon almond
essence

1¼ cups Edmonds standard flour
70 g packet ground almonds
icing sugar to dust

Cream butter and sugar until light and fluffy. Beat in essence. Sift flour. Fold flour and ground almonds into creamed mixture. Spoon mixture into a piping bag fitted with a 1 cm-diameter star nozzle. Pipe small crescent shapes onto lightly greased oven trays. Bake at 160°C for 25 minutes. Cool biscuits on trays. Five minutes after removing from the oven, dust biscuits lightly with icing sugar. Makes 38 biscuits.

American Chocolate Brownies (Top left)
Anzac Biscuits (Top right)
Almond Biscuits (Left)
Almond Crescent Biscuits (Right)

AMERICAN CHOCOLATE BROWNIES

175 g butter
250 g cooking chocolate
1½ cups Edmonds standard flour
1 cup sugar
2 teaspoons vanilla essence
3 eggs, beaten
icing sugar to dust

CHOCOLATE ICING (see page 11)
1 cup walnuts, chopped (optional)

In a medium-sized saucepan, melt butter and chocolate over a low heat. Remove saucepan from the heat and add flour, sugar, vanilla and eggs. Stir until well combined. Pour mixture into a 20 cm square tin lined on the base with baking paper. Bake at 180°C for 40 minutes. Leave in tin for 10 minutes before turning out onto a wire rack. When cold, dust with icing sugar, or ice with Chocolate Icing and top with chopped walnuts. Cut into squares.

ANZAC BISCUITS

½ cup Edmonds standard flour

½ cup sugar

¾ cup coconut

¾ cup rolled oats

100 g butter

1 tablespoon golden syrup

½ teaspoon Edmonds baking soda

2 tablespoons boiling water

Mix together flour, sugar, coconut and rolled oats. Melt butter and golden syrup. Dissolve baking soda in the boiling water and add to butter and golden syrup. Stir butter mixture into the dry ingredients. Place level tablespoons of mixture 4–5 cm apart on cold greased oven trays. Bake at 180°C for about 15 minutes or until golden. Makes 22.

BASIC BISCUITS (WITH VARIATIONS)

BASIC BISCUITS
125 g butter, softened
¾ cup sugar
1 teaspoon vanilla essence
1 egg
2 cups Edmonds standard flour
1 teaspoon Edmonds baking powder

Cream butter, sugar and vanilla together until light and fluffy. Add egg, beating well. Sift flour and baking powder together and mix into creamed mixture. Roll heaped teaspoons of mixture into balls and place on an oven tray. Flatten slightly with a floured fork. Bake at 190°C for about 12 minutes or until pale golden. Makes about 35.

CHOCOLATE BISCUITS
Add 2 tablespoons of cocoa when sifting flour.

SULTANA BISCUITS
Fold ½ cup of sultanas into creamed mixture.

SPICE BISCUITS
Add 2 teaspoons of mixed spice when sifting flour.

LEMON BISCUITS
Omit vanilla essence and add 2 teaspoons of grated lemon zest to creamed mixture.

ORANGE BISCUITS
Omit vanilla essence and add 1 tablespoon of grated orange zest to creamed mixture.

Basic Biscuits (with chocolate variation pictured)

BISCOTTI

2 cups Edmonds standard flour
2 teaspoons Edmonds baking powder
pinch of salt
¾ cup caster sugar
1 teaspoon almond essence
3 eggs
finely grated zest of 1 orange
½ cup chopped, toasted almonds

Sift flour, baking powder and salt into a bowl. Mix in caster sugar. Lightly beat almond essence, eggs and orange zest together. Mix with dry ingredients and almonds until well combined. The dough should be firm. Add more flour if necessary. Shape into a log about 30 cm long. Place on a greased oven tray and flatten the log with the palm of your hand. Bake at 180°C for 35 minutes or until cooked. Cool for 10 minutes then cut log into 1 cm slices on the diagonal. Place slices on an oven tray. Bake at 150°C for 20 minutes or until biscotti are dry and crisp. Store in an airtight container.
Makes about 30.

CARAMEL MERINGUE

BASE
75 g butter, softened
1½ tablespoons sugar
1 egg
1 cup Edmonds standard
flour
1 teaspoon Edmonds
baking powder
pinch of salt

FILLING
1 tablespoon butter
2 tablespoons Edmonds
standard flour
½ cup brown sugar
½ tin sweetened condensed milk
1 tablespoon golden syrup
1 teaspoon vanilla essence
2 egg yolks

MERINGUE
2 egg whites
¼ cup caster sugar

Cream butter and sugar, add egg and beat well. Add sifted flour, baking powder and salt. Press into a 30 x 20 cm sponge-roll tin lined on the base with baking paper. Bake 10 to 15 minutes at 190°C. To make the filling, melt butter in a saucepan. Add flour and cook until frothy. Stir in brown sugar, condensed milk, golden syrup, vanilla and egg yolks. Stir continuously over a medium heat for 1 minute. Cool. Spread cold filling over base. Top with meringue. To make the meringue, beat egg whites until stiff. Gradually add caster sugar and continue beating until stiff and glossy. Bake at 160°C for 20–25 minutes. Cut while hot.

Chinese Chews (Top left)
Caramel Meringue (Top centre)
Chocolate Caramel Slice (Left and top right)
Chocolate Rough (Right)

CHINESE CHEWS

2 eggs

1 cup brown sugar

75 g butter, melted

1 teaspoon vanilla essence

1½ cups Edmonds standard flour

1 teaspoon Edmonds baking powder

pinch of salt

½ cup rolled oats

¾ cup chopped dates

¾ cup chopped walnuts

¾ cup crystallised ginger

Beat eggs and brown sugar until well mixed. Add butter and vanilla. Sift flour, baking powder and salt into a large bowl. Stir in rolled oats. Pour egg mixture into the sifted dry ingredients. Add dates, walnuts and ginger. Mix well. Spread mixture into a 23 cm square cake tin lined on the base with baking paper. Bake at 180°C for 30–35 minutes or until cooked. Cut into squares while still hot.

CHOCOLATE CARAMEL SLICE

150 g butter
1 tablespoon golden syrup
½ cup brown sugar
1 cup Edmonds standard flour
1 teaspoon Edmonds
baking powder
1 cup rolled oats

CARAMEL ICING
1 cup brown sugar
2 tablespoons sweetened
condensed milk
2 tablespoons butter
1 cup icing sugar
1 tablespoon hot water

CHOCOLATE ICING (see page 11)

Melt butter, golden syrup and brown sugar in a saucepan large enough to mix all the ingredients. Mix in flour, baking powder and rolled oats until combined. Press into a shallow 20 cm square tin lined on the base with baking paper. Bake at 180°C for 15 minutes. Spread with warm Caramel Icing and top with Chocolate Icing. To make the Caramel Icing, place brown sugar, condensed milk and butter in a saucepan. Heat until bubbling and remove from heat. Add icing sugar and water. Beat to combine. Allow icing to set before cutting into squares or fingers.

CHOCOLATE ROUGH

120 g butter

⅓ cup caster sugar

½ cup coconut

1 cup Edmonds Self
Rising flour

2 teaspoons cocoa

pinch of salt

TOPPING

25 g butter

3 tablespoons sweetened
condensed milk

1 tablespoon cocoa

1 cup icing sugar

1 cup coconut

1 teaspoon vanilla essence

a little boiling water

Place butter in a medium microwave-proof bowl. Cover and melt on High (100%) for 1–1½ minutes. Stir in remaining ingredients. Press into a square microwave-proof baking dish and cook on Medium (70%) for about 5½ minutes, or until just firm. Cool slightly. Spread with topping while still warm. To make the topping, place butter in a microwave-proof bowl. Cover and melt on High for 40–50 seconds. Stir in remaining ingredients, adding sufficient hot water to mix to a spreadable consistency. Allow icing to set before cutting into slices.

COCONUT AND ALMOND SLICE

250 g packet plain sweet
biscuits, crushed
¾ cup chopped toasted blanched
almonds
1 cup coconut
finely grated zest and
juice of 1 lemon
2 drops almond essence
100 g butter

½ cup sweetened
condensed milk

LEMON ICING
1½ cups icing sugar
2 tablespoons butter
1 teaspoon lemon juice
boiling water to mix

Combine biscuit crumbs, almonds, coconut, lemon zest, juice and essence in a bowl. Place butter and condensed milk in a small saucepan. Stir over a low heat until the butter melts. Pour over biscuit mixture. Mix well. Press over the base of a 25 cm x 20 cm shallow baking dish. Refrigerate for 1 hour until firm. To make the icing, combine all ingredients in a bowl, adding sufficient boiling water to mix to a stiff paste. Spread over slice. Refrigerate for 1 hour or until set. Store in the refrigerator.

COFFEE KISSES

250 g butter, softened
¾ cup icing sugar
3 teaspoons instant coffee powder
2 teaspoons milk
2 cups Edmonds standard flour
½ cup Edmonds Fielder's cornflour

COFFEE ICING
1 cup icing sugar
1 teaspoon instant coffee powder
2 teaspoons melted butter
milk to mix

Cream butter and icing sugar until light and fluffy. Dissolve coffee in milk. Add to creamed mixture and beat well. Sift flour and cornflour. Stir into creamed mixture. Spoon mixture into a piping bag fitted with a 2 cm-diameter star nozzle. Pipe 4 cm-diameter rosettes onto greased oven trays, allowing a little room for spreading. Bake at 180°C for 15–18 minutes. Cool on oven trays. Sandwich biscuits together with Coffee Icing. To make the icing, combine icing sugar and coffee in a bowl. Stir in butter and sufficient milk to mix to a spreadable consistency.
Makes 14 kisses.

COFFEE WALNUT SLICE

BASE

175 g butter, softened

1 egg

2 cups Edmonds standard flour

½ cup caster sugar

**¾ teaspoon Edmonds
baking powder**

FILLING

**395 g can sweetened
condensed milk**

2 tablespoons butter

2 tablespoons golden syrup

2 teaspoons coffee essence

¾ cup roughly chopped walnuts

TOPPING

125 g butter, softened

½ cup caster sugar

1 cup Edmonds standard flour

1 teaspoon cinnamon

To make the base, beat butter, egg, flour, caster sugar and baking powder to a soft dough using an electric mixer. Press over the base of a greased 25 cm-square shallow baking tin. Prick all over with a fork. Bake at 180°C for 20–25 minutes until golden. While the base is cooking, prepare the filling. Place all filling ingredients in a saucepan. Stir over a low heat for 4–5 minutes until the mixture thickens. Remove from heat and cool slightly. To make the topping, beat all ingredients together for 1 minute with an electric mixer. Form into a ball and cover with plastic wrap. Refrigerate for at least 10 minutes. Spread the cooled filling over the cooked base. Coarsely grate topping-dough over filling. Bake for 25–30 minutes until golden. Cool before cutting into slices.

Ginger Biscuits (Top left)
Duskies (Top right)
Coffee Walnut Slice (Centre)

DUSKIES

125 g butter, softened
1 cup icing sugar
1 egg
1¼ cups Edmonds standard flour
2 tablespoons cocoa
1 teaspoon Edmonds baking powder
½ cup coconut
½ cup chopped walnuts

CHOCOLATE ICING (see page 11)

Cream butter and icing sugar, add egg then beat. Sift in flour, cocoa and baking powder. Add coconut and walnuts. Mix and place in small spoonfuls on cold, greased trays. Bake at 200°C for 12–15 minutes. When cold, ice with Chocolate Icing and decorate with coconut.
Makes 36.

GINGER BISCUITS

200 g butter, softened
¾ cup caster sugar
¼ cup golden syrup
2¼ cups Edmonds standard flour
2 teaspoons Edmonds baking soda
1 tablespoon ground ginger

Cream butter and caster sugar until light and fluffy. Add golden syrup and beat well. Sift dry ingredients. Stir into creamed mixture to form a soft dough. Roll heaped teaspoons of mixture into balls. Place 3–4 cm apart on greased oven trays. Bake at 160°C for 30 minutes. Cool on wire racks.
Makes 38 biscuits.

GINGER CRUNCH

125 g butter, softened
½ cup sugar
1½ cups Edmonds standard flour
1 teaspoon Edmonds baking powder
1 teaspoon ground ginger

GINGER ICING
75 g butter
¾ cup icing sugar
2 tablespoons golden syrup
3 teaspoons ground ginger

Cream butter and sugar until light and fluffy. Sift flour, baking powder and ginger together. Mix into creamed mixture. Turn dough out onto a lightly floured board. Knead well. Press dough into a greased 20 x 30 cm sponge-roll tin. Bake at 190°C for 20–25 minutes or until golden. Pour hot Ginger Icing over base while hot and cut into squares while still warm. To make the Ginger Icing, combine butter, icing sugar, golden syrup and ginger in a small saucepan. Heat until butter is melted, stirring constantly.

HOKEY POKEY BISCUITS

125 g butter
½ cup sugar
1 tablespoon golden syrup
1 tablespoon milk
1½ cups Edmonds standard flour
1 teaspoon Edmonds baking soda

Combine butter, sugar, golden syrup and milk in a saucepan. Heat until butter is melted and mixture nearly boiling, stirring constantly. Remove from heat and allow mixture to cool to lukewarm. Sift flour and baking soda together. Add to the cooled mixture. Stir well. Roll tablespoons of mixture into balls and place on ungreased oven trays. Flatten with a floured fork. Bake at 180°C for 15–20 minutes or until golden brown.
Makes 22.

HONEY NUT BARS

BASE
1½ cups Edmonds standard flour
½ teaspoon Edmonds baking powder
¼ cup icing sugar
150 g butter, softened
2 egg yolks

TOPPING
75 g butter
⅓ cup runny honey
⅓ cup sugar
¾ cup hazelnuts
½ cup blanched almonds
½ cup walnut pieces
½ cup pecan nuts

To make the base, place flour, baking powder, icing sugar and butter in a food processor. Pulse until mixture is crumbly. Add egg yolks and pulse until mixture comes together. Press over the base of a 27 cm x 18 cm shallow baking tin that has been lined with baking paper and greased. Prick the base several times with a fork. Bake at 180°C for 15 minutes until golden. To make the topping, place butter, honey and sugar in a saucepan. Stir over a low heat until sugar dissolves. Bring to the boil. Simmer for 2 minutes. Remove from heat and stir in nuts. Spread topping evenly over the base. Bake for 20 minutes. Cool, then cut into bars. During warmer weather, keep in the refrigerator.

HONEY SNAPS

50 g butter
2 tablespoons sugar
3 tablespoons honey
½ cup Edmonds standard flour
1 teaspoon Edmonds baking powder
½ teaspoon ground ginger

Melt butter, sugar and honey together in a saucepan. Remove from heat. Add flour, baking powder, ginger and stir until mixture is smooth. Drop teaspoons of mixture onto a cold oven tray, leaving enough room for mixture to spread to double its size. Bake at 180°C for 10 minutes or until golden. Leave on tray for a few minutes to cool before removing to a wire rack.
Makes 20.

Lemon Oaty Squares (Top left)
Honey Snaps (Left)
Lemon Slice (Right)

LEMON OATY SQUARES

100 g butter	**ICING**
¼ cup brown sugar	**25 g butter**
¼ cup caster sugar	**1 tablespoon water**
2 cups rolled oats	**1 tablespoon lemon juice**
¼ cup Edmonds standard flour	**1 teaspoon grated lemon zest**
½ cup coconut	**about 1½ cups icing sugar**
½ cup chocolate chips	

Place butter and sugars into a microwave-proof bowl. Cover and cook on High (100%) for 1–1½ minutes, or until butter has melted. Stir to combine. Add rolled oats, flour, coconut and chocolate chips. Mix well. Press into an 18 x 22 cm glass microwave-proof slice dish. Cook elevated on a microwave-proof rack, on High for 2½–3½ minutes, or until bubbling all over, taking care that the middle does not start to burn. Spread slice with Lemon Icing. To make the icing, place butter, water, lemon juice and zest in a 1 litre microwave-proof jug. Cook on High for 1–1½ minutes or until just boiling. Add the icing sugar, beating well to form a soft, spreadable icing. Allow icing to cool before cutting into squares.

LEMON SLICE

150 g butter
1½ cups Edmonds standard flour
½ cup icing sugar

TOPPING
2 tablespoons Edmonds custard powder
½ teaspoon Edmonds baking powder
1 cup sugar
½ cup lemon juice
1 tablespoon grated lemon zest
3 eggs

Melt the butter. Remove from heat and mix in flour and icing sugar. Press into the base of a greased 20 x 30 cm sponge-roll tin lined with baking paper. Bake at 180°C for 15–20 minutes or until lightly golden. To make the topping, mix custard powder, baking powder, sugar, lemon juice, lemon zest and eggs together until combined. Pour topping over base and bake for a further 25 minutes or until set. Cut into slices when cold.

LEMON STAR BISCUITS

125 g butter, softened

¾ cup caster sugar

1 egg

2 teaspoons finely grated lemon zest

2 cups Edmonds standard flour

LEMON ICING

1 cup icing sugar

2 teaspoons butter

1 tablespoon lemon juice

boiling water to mix

silver balls to decorate (optional)

Cream butter and caster sugar until light and fluffy. Add egg and lemon zest. Beat well. Sift flour. Stir into creamed mixture, mixing to a soft dough. Shape dough into a ball. Cover with plastic wrap and refrigerate for 30 minutes. Roll dough out on a floured surface to a thickness of 5 mm. Using a star-shaped biscuit cutter, stamp out shapes. Place on greased oven trays. Bake at 180°C for 12 minutes until lightly golden. Cool on wire racks. When cold, spread with lemon icing and decorate with silver balls. Alternatively, dust with icing sugar just before serving.

LOUISE CAKE

150 g butter, softened
¼ cup sugar
4 eggs, separated
2 cups Edmonds standard flour
2 teaspoons Edmonds

baking powder
¼ cup raspberry jam
½ cup caster sugar
½ cup coconut

Cream butter and sugar until light and fluffy. Beat in egg yolks. Sift flour and baking powder together. Stir into creamed mixture. Press dough into a greased 20 x 30 cm sponge-roll tin lined on the base with baking paper. Spread raspberry jam over the base. Using an electric mixer, beat egg whites until soft peaks form. Gradually add caster sugar, beating continuously. Beat until glossy. Fold in coconut. Spread meringue mixture over jam. Bake at 180°C for 30 minutes or until meringue is dry and lightly coloured. Cut into squares while still warm.

MACADAMIA NUT AND WHITE CHOCOLATE BISCUITS

200 g butter, softened
1 cup caster sugar
2 eggs
1 teaspoon vanilla essence
3 cups Edmonds standard flour
2 teaspoons Edmonds baking powder
100 g chopped white chocolate
⅓ cup chopped macadamia nuts

Cream butter and caster sugar until light and fluffy. Add eggs one at a time, beating well after each addition. Beat in essence. Sift flour and baking powder. Stir into creamed mixture along with chocolate and nuts. Take heaped teaspoons of mixture and roll into balls. Place on greased oven trays, allowing room for spreading. Flatten slightly with a floured fork. Bake at 180°C for 15–18 minutes until golden. Cool on wire racks. Makes 40 biscuits.

MELTING MOMENTS

200 g butter, softened
¾ cup icing sugar
1 cup Edmonds standard flour
1 cup Edmonds Fielder's cornflour
½ teaspoon Edmonds baking powder

VANILLA ICING (or raspberry jam)
1 cup icing sugar
¼ teaspoon vanilla essence
1 teaspoon butter
a little boiling water to mix

Cream butter and icing sugar until light and fluffy. Sift flour, cornflour and baking powder. Add to creamed mixture, mixing well. Roll dough into small balls (the size of large marbles) and place on a greased oven tray. Flatten slightly with a floured fork. Bake at 180°C for 20 minutes. Cool on wire racks. Sandwich two biscuits together with Vanilla Icing or raspberry jam. To make the Vanilla Icing, place icing sugar, vanilla essence and butter in a bowl. Add sufficient water to mix to a spreadable consistency.
Makes 16.

MUNCHKIN BARS

1 cup brown sugar

100 g butter

½ cup apricot jam

¼ cup golden syrup

3 cups rolled oats

1 cup pumpkin kernels

1 teaspoon mixed spice

½ cup sesame seeds

½ cup coconut

1 teaspoon vanilla essence

1 cup sultanas (optional)

In a saucepan, melt together the brown sugar, butter, apricot jam and golden syrup. Combine the rest of the ingredients in a large bowl. Pour in melted mixture. Mix well. Press mixture firmly into a greased 20 x 30 cm sponge-roll tin that has been lined with baking paper on the base. Bake at 180°C for 25 minutes or until golden. Cool slightly and cut into bars.

Oat Biscuits (Top left)
Peanut Brownies (Top right)
Munchkin Bars (Centre)

The next day was Saturday. M
and went off to buy her C

OAT BISCUITS

125 g butter, softened
½ cup sugar
2 tablespoons honey
1 cup Edmonds standard flour
1 teaspoon Edmonds baking powder
½ teaspoon cinnamon
1½ cups rolled oats

Cream butter, sugar and honey together until pale. Sift flour, baking powder and cinnamon together. Add sifted dry ingredients and rolled oats to creamed mixture, stirring well. Roll tablespoons of mixture into balls. Place on a greased oven tray. Flatten with a floured fork and bake at 180°C for 15 minutes or until golden. Transfer to a wire rack to cool.
Makes 30.

PEANUT BROWNIES

125 g butter, softened

1 cup sugar

1 egg

1½ cups Edmonds standard flour

1 teaspoon Edmonds baking powder

pinch of salt

2 tablespoons cocoa

1 cup blanched peanuts, roasted

Cream butter and sugar until light and fluffy. Add egg and beat well. Sift flour, baking powder, salt and cocoa together. Mix into creamed mixture. Add cold peanuts and mix well. Roll tablespoons of mixture into balls. Place on greased oven trays. Flatten with a floured fork. Bake at 180°C for 15 minutes or until cooked.
Makes 35.

REFRIGERATED APRICOT AND LEMON SLICE

125 g butter

½ cup sweetened condensed milk

250 g packet malt biscuits, crushed

1 cup dried apricots, finely chopped

1 teaspoon grated lemon zest

1 cup coconut

LEMON ICING

2 cups icing sugar

1 teaspoon butter

1 teaspoon grated lemon zest

a little boiling water

3 tablespoons coconut

Place butter and condensed milk in a small saucepan. Stir over a low heat until butter has melted. Combine biscuit crumbs, apricots, lemon zest and first measure of coconut in a bowl. Add butter mixture and stir until well combined. Press into a greased 20 cm x 30 cm sponge-roll tin. Refrigerate for 1 hour. Ice with Lemon Icing and sprinkle with second measure of coconut. To make the Lemon Icing, combine icing sugar, butter and lemon zest in a bowl. Add sufficient boiling water to mix to a spreadable consistency. Allow icing to set before cutting into squares.

ROCKY ROAD SLICE

BASE
1 cup Edmonds standard flour
½ teaspoon Edmonds baking powder
3 tablespoons cocoa
¾ cup caster sugar
¾ cup coconut
125 g butter, melted
1 egg

TOPPING
250 g dark chocolate, chopped
(or melts or bits)
2 tablespoons Kremelta
25 marshmallows
½ cup toasted coconut
½ cup pistachio nuts (or chopped walnuts)

Sift flour, baking powder and cocoa into a bowl. Stir in caster sugar and coconut. Add butter and egg and mix well. Spread over the base of a greased 27 cm x 18 cm shallow baking tin. Bake at 180°C for 20–25 minutes. Cool for 15 minutes, then spread with topping. To make the topping, place chocolate and Kremelta in a heatproof bowl. Sit over a saucepan of simmering water. Stir continuously until chocolate and Kremelta have melted and the mixture is smooth. Set aside for 5 minutes to cool slightly. Add marshmallows, coconut and nuts to melted chocolate. Mix well. Spread over warm base. Allow topping to set before cutting into pieces. NB: During warm weather, refrigerate slice for setting and keep in the refrigerator.

SANTE BISCUITS

125 g butter, softened
¼ cup sugar
3 tablespoons sweetened condensed milk
few drops vanilla essence
1½ cups Edmonds standard flour
1 teaspoon Edmonds baking powder
½ cup chocolate chips

Cream butter, sugar, condensed milk and vanilla until light and fluffy. Sift flour and baking powder together. Mix sifted dry ingredients and chocolate chips into creamed mixture. Roll tablespoons of mixture into balls. Place on a greased oven tray and flatten with a floured fork. Bake at 180°C for 20 minutes.
Makes 25.

Shortbread (Top left)
Sante Biscuits (Left)
Yoghurt Raisin biscuits (Right)

SHORTBREAD

250 g butter, softened
1 cup icing sugar
1 cup Edmonds Fielder's cornflour
2 cups Edmonds standard flour

Cream butter and icing sugar until light and fluffy. Sift cornflour and flour together. Mix sifted ingredients into creamed mixture. Knead well. Divide dough into two equal portions and form into logs 6 cm across and 2 cm in depth. Cover with plastic wrap and refrigerate for 1 hour. Cut into 1 cm thick slices. Place on greased oven trays. Prick with a fork. Bake at 180°C for 15–20 minutes or until a pale golden colour. Makes about 35.

YOGHURT RAISIN BISCUITS

125 g butter

½ cup sugar

1 egg

1 teaspoon vanilla essence

¾ cup yoghurt-covered raisins

2 cups Edmonds standard flour

1½ teaspoons Edmonds baking powder

Melt butter. Cool slightly. Using a wooden spoon, beat sugar and egg together for 2 minutes, until thick and pale. Add butter and mix well. Stir in essence and raisins. Sift flour and baking powder. Stir into liquid ingredients. Take heaped teaspoons of mixture and form into balls. Place 3–4 cm apart on greased oven trays. Flatten slightly with the palm of your hand. Bake at 180°C for 15 minutes until golden. Cool on wire racks.

Makes about 25.

CAKES

ALMOND CRUMBLE CAKE

125 g butter, softened

¾ cup caster sugar

2 eggs

¼ teaspoon almond essence

1½ cups Edmonds standard flour

2 teaspoons Edmonds baking powder

70 g packet ground almonds

1 cup milk

CRUMBLE TOPPING

½ cup Edmonds standard flour

2 tablespoons brown sugar

70 g packet sliced almonds

¼ cup melted butter

Cream butter and sugar until light and fluffy. Add eggs one at a time, beating well after each addition. Beat in almond essence. Sift together flour and baking powder. Fold into creamed mixture alternately with ground almonds and milk. Spoon into a greased 20 cm round cake tin that has the base lined with baking paper. Scatter crumble topping over cake. To make the topping, combine all ingredients in a bowl. Mix well. Bake at 180°C for 50–55 minutes or until a skewer inserted in the centre of the cake comes out clean. Leave cake in tin for 15 minutes before turning onto a wire rack.

Almond Crumble Cake (top centre)
Butter Cake (left)
Banana Cake (right)

BANANA CAKE

125 g butter, softened

¾ cup sugar

2 eggs

1½ cups mashed ripe banana (about 4 medium bananas)

1 teaspoon Edmonds baking soda

2 tablespoons hot milk

2 cups Edmonds standard flour

1 teaspoon Edmonds baking powder

LEMON ICING (see page 112)

lemon zest to garnish

Cream butter and sugar until light and fluffy. Add eggs one at a time, beating well after each addition. Add mashed banana and mix thoroughly. Stir soda into hot milk and add to creamed mixture. Sift flour and baking powder. Fold into mixture. Turn into a greased and lined 20 cm round cake tin. Bake at 180°C for 50 minutes or until cake springs back when lightly touched. Leave in tin for 10 minutes before turning out onto a wire rack. When cold, ice with Lemon Icing and garnish with lemon zest.

VARIATION

The mixture can be baked in two 20 cm round sandwich tins at 180°C for 25 minutes. The two cakes can be filled with whipped cream and sliced banana.

BUTTER CAKE

150 g butter, softened
1 teaspoon vanilla essence
¾ cup sugar
2 eggs
1½ cups Edmonds standard flour
3 teaspoons Edmonds baking powder
¾ cup milk, approximately
icing sugar to dust

Cream butter, vanilla and sugar until light and fluffy. Add eggs one at a time, beating well after each addition. Sift flour and baking powder together. Fold into creamed mixture. Add sufficient milk to give a soft dropping consistency. Spoon mixture into a greased and lined deep 20 cm round cake tin. Bake at 180°°C for 35–40 minutes or until cake springs back when lightly touched. Leave in tin for 10 minutes before turning out onto a wire rack. When cold, dust with icing sugar.

CAPPUCCINO CAKE

150 g butter

¾ cup sugar

3 egg yolks

1½ cups Edmonds standard flour

2 teaspoons Edmonds baking powder

½ cup strong black coffee, cooled

1 teaspoon cinnamon

TOPPING

3 egg whites

¾ cup caster sugar

Melt butter in a saucepan large enough to mix all the ingredients. Remove from heat and stir in sugar and egg yolks. Fold in sifted flour and baking powder alternately with coffee. Place mixture in a 20 cm round springform tin lined on the base with baking paper. Spread topping over. To make the topping, beat egg whites until stiff. Gradually beat in sugar and continue beating until mixture is thick. Bake at 180°C for 45–50 minutes or until an inserted skewer comes out clean. Cool in tin before releasing the sides of the tin. Cool. Dust with cinnamon.

CARROT CAKE

3 eggs

1 cup sugar

¾ cup vegetable oil

2 cups Edmonds standard flour

1 teaspoon Edmonds baking powder

1 teaspoon Edmonds baking soda

½ teaspoon cinnamon

3 cups grated carrots

¾ cup (225 g can) drained unsweetened crushed pineapple

½ cup chopped walnuts

1 teaspoon grated orange rind (optional)

CREAM CHEESE ICING (see page 112)

orange zest to garnish

Beat together eggs and sugar for 5 minutes until thick. Add oil and beat for 1 minute. Sift flour, baking powder, baking soda and cinnamon. Combine carrot, pineapple, walnuts and orange rind. Fold into egg mixture. Fold in dry ingredients. Grease a deep 20 cm ring tin. Line base with baking paper. Spoon mixture into tin. Bake at 180°C for 50–55 minutes or until a skewer inserted in the centre of the cake comes out clean. Leave in tin for 10 minutes before turning out onto a wire rack. When cold, spread with Cream Cheese Icing and garnish with orange zest.

CHOCOLATE CAKE

(WITH BLACK FOREST VARIATION PHOTOGRAPHED)

175 g butter, softened

1 teaspoon vanilla essence

1¾ cups sugar

3 eggs

2 cups Edmonds standard flour

½ cup cocoa

2 teaspoons Edmonds baking powder

1 cup milk

CHOCOLATE ICING (see page 112)

Cream butter, vanilla essence and sugar until light and fluffy. Add eggs one at a time, beating well after each addition. Sift together cocoa, flour and baking powder. Fold into creamed mixture alternately with milk. Spoon mixture into a greased and lined 22 cm round cake tin. Bake at 180°C for 55–60 minutes or until a skewer inserted in the centre comes out clean. Leave in tin for 10 minutes before turning out onto a wire rack. When cold, ice with Chocolate Icing or dust with icing sugar.

BLACK FOREST CAKE

CHOCOLATE CAKE (recipe above)

CHOCOLATE GANACHE

100 g dark chocolate, chopped

2 tablespoons cream

¼ cup Kirsch

250 ml cream, whipped

425 g can stoneless black cherries, thoroughly drained

To make the ganache, place chocolate and cream in a small saucepan. Stir over a low heat until chocolate has melted and the mixture is smooth. Cool. Cut cake horizontally into 3 layers. Place one layer on a serving plate. Brush liberally with Kirsch. Spread with half the cream then arrange half the cherries on top. Repeat with another layer of cake, Kirsch, cream and cherries. Top with final layer of cake. Spread ganache over top of cake.

CHOCOLATE CHERRY BRANDY CAKE

425 g can stoneless black
cherries, drained and halved
¼ cup brandy
2 tablespoons brown sugar
100 g dark cooking chocolate,
coarsely chopped
175 g butter, softened
1 cup sugar
3 eggs
2 cups Edmonds high
grade flour

2 tablespoons cocoa
2 teaspoons Edmonds
baking powder
¼ cup milk

CHOCOLATE ICING
100 g dark cooking
chocolate, chopped
50 g butter

Combine cherries, brandy, brown sugar and chocolate. Set aside to marinate while preparing the cake. Cream the butter and sugar until light and fluffy. Add eggs one at a time, beating well after each addition. Sift flour, baking powder and cocoa together. Fold into creamed mixture alternately with milk. Gently fold in cherries and chocolate mixture. Spoon mixture into a greased and lightly floured 23 cm gugelhupf (ribbed ring tin) or a deep 23 cm ring tin. Bake at 180°C for 45 minutes or until cake springs back when lightly touched. Leave cake in tin for 10 minutes before turning out onto a wire rack. When cool, dribble hot Chocolate Icing over the cake using a spoon. To make the icing, melt the chocolate and butter together over a pot of hot water, stirring constantly until smooth.

CHOCOLATE CHIP SPECKLE CAKE

175 g butter, softened

1½ cups sugar

4 eggs

1 teaspoon vanilla essence

1½ cups Edmonds standard flour

1½ teaspoons Edmonds baking powder

¾ cup chocolate chips

Cream butter and sugar until light and fluffy. Add eggs one at a time, beating well after each addition. Beat in vanilla. Sift together flour and baking powder. Fold into creamed mixture with chocolate chips. Spoon mixture into a well-greased 22 cm baba tin. Bake at 180°C for 55–60 minutes or until a skewer inserted in the centre of the cake comes out clean. Leave cake in tin for 10 minutes before turning onto a wire rack.

CINNAMON PECAN CAKE

100 g pecan nuts
125 g butter, softened
1 cup caster sugar
2 eggs
1 teaspoon vanilla essence
1½ cups Edmonds standard
flour
1½ teaspoons Edmonds
baking powder

1 teaspoon cinnamon
¾ cup milk

COFFEE CREAM FILLING
75 g butter, softened
1 cup icing sugar
1 teaspoon instant coffee
icing sugar to dust

Place pecan nuts in a food processor. Pulse until ground. Cream butter and sugar until light and fluffy. Add eggs one at a time, beating well after each addition. Beat in vanilla. Fold in ground pecans. Sift together flour, baking powder and cinnamon. Fold into creamed mixture alternately with milk. Spoon into a greased 20 cm round cake tin that has had the base lined with baking paper. Bake at 180°C for 45 minutes, or until a skewer inserted in the centre of the cake comes out clean. Leave cake in tin for 10 minutes before turning onto a wire rack. When cold, split cake in half horizontally. Place one half on a serving plate. Spread over Coffee Cream Filling then sandwich with remaining half of cake. To make the filling, beat together butter, icing sugar and coffee until smooth. Dust cake with icing sugar. If desired, cut star shapes out of baking paper and place on top of the cake before dusting with icing sugar.

Coconut Cake (top)
Citrus Sour Cream Cake (below left)
Cinnamon Pecan Cake (below right)

CITRUS SOUR CREAM CAKE

125 g butter, softened

1 teaspoon grated lemon rind

1 teaspoon grated orange rind

1 cup sugar

3 eggs

1 cup Edmonds standard flour

1 teaspoon Edmonds baking powder

½ cup sour cream

tiny citrus leaves and orange rind to garnish

Cream butter, lemon rind, orange rind and sugar together until light and fluffy. Add eggs one at a time and beat well. Sift flour and baking powder together. Fold sifted ingredients into egg mixture alternately with sour cream, mixing until smooth. Pour mixture into a greased 20 cm round cake tin lined on the base with baking paper. Bake at 160°C for 45 minutes or until cake springs back when lightly touched. Leave in tin for 10 minutes before turning out onto a wire rack. Garnish with tiny citrus leaves and orange rind.

COCONUT CAKE

250 g butter, softened
1½ cups caster sugar
4 eggs
1 teaspoon vanilla essence
2 cups Edmonds standard flour
2 teaspoons Edmonds baking powder
1 cup desiccated coconut

WHITE ICING (see page 112)
toasted thread coconut to garnish

Cream butter and sugar until light and fluffy. Add eggs one at a time, beating well after each addition. Beat in vanilla essence. Sift together flour and baking powder. Fold flour and coconut into creamed mixture. Spoon into a greased deep 24 cm ring tin that has had the base lined with baking paper. Bake at 180°C for 45 minutes or until a skewer inserted in the cake comes out clean. Leave cake in tin for 10 minutes before turning onto a wire rack. When cold, spread with White Icing and garnish with toasted coconut.

COFFEE CAKE

250 g butter, softened
1½ cups caster sugar
3 eggs
2 cups Edmonds standard flour
2 teaspoons Edmonds baking powder
2 tablespoons coffee essence
¾ cup milk

COFFEE ICING (see page 112)

Cream butter and sugar until light and fluffy. Add eggs one at a time, beating well after each addition. Sift together flour and baking powder. Combine essence and milk. Fold dry ingredients and milk alternately into creamed mixture. Spoon into a deep 22 cm round cake tin that has had the base lined with baking paper. Bake at 180°C for 50–55 minutes or until a skewer inserted in the centre of the cake comes out clean. Leave cake in tin for 10 minutes before turning onto a wire rack. When cold, spread with Coffee Icing.

CONTINENTAL APPLE CAKE

250 g butter, melted

1¼ cups sugar

3¼ cups Edmonds standard flour

6 teaspoons Edmonds baking powder

4 eggs

2 large Granny Smith apples, peeled, cored and sliced

½ cup sultanas

2 tablespoons sugar

2 teaspoons cinnamon

1 teaspoon almond essence

icing sugar to dust

whipped cream or yoghurt to serve

Put butter, first measure of sugar, flour, baking powder and eggs into a bowl. Beat with an electric mixer on high speed until smooth. In a separate bowl combine apple slices, sultanas, second measure of sugar, cinnamon and almond essence. Spoon two-thirds of the batter into a greased and lined 25 cm round cake tin. Arrange the apple mixture on top. Spoon remaining batter over apple mixture. Bake at 180°C for 40–45 minutes or until cake is risen and golden. Leave in tin for 10 minutes before turning out onto a wire rack. Dust with icing sugar. Serve with cream or yoghurt.

DATE LOAF

1 cup chopped dates
1 cup boiling water
1 teaspoon Edmonds baking soda
1 tablespoon butter
1 cup brown sugar
1 egg, beaten
1 cup chopped walnuts
¼ teaspoon vanilla essence
2 cups Edmonds standard flour
1 teaspoon Edmonds baking powder

Put dates, water, soda and butter into a bowl. Stir until butter has melted. Set aside for 1 hour. Beat sugar, egg, walnuts and vanilla into date mixture. Sift flour and baking powder into date mixture, stirring just to combine. Pour mixture into a greased 22 cm loaf tin. Bake at 180°C for 45 minutes or until loaf springs back when lightly touched. Leave in tin for 10 minutes before turning onto a wire rack.

FIELDER'S SPONGE

3 no. 7 eggs, separated
½ cup caster sugar
½ cup Edmonds Fielder's cornflour
2 teaspoons Edmonds standard flour
1 teaspoon Edmonds baking powder

Beat egg whites until stiff. Gradually add the sugar, beating continuously until mixture is stiff and sugar has dissolved. Add egg yolks and beat well. Sift cornflour, flour and baking powder. Carefully fold into egg mixture with a metal spoon. Pour into two 20 cm sandwich tins lined on the base with baking paper. Bake at 190°C for 15–20 minutes or until cake springs back when lightly touched. Leave in tin for 5 minutes before turning out onto a wire rack.

Serving suggestion: Sandwich sponges together with whipped cream and hulled, halved strawberries. Dust with icing sugar.

Lemon Curd and Yoghurt Cake (top)
Fruit Cake (below left)
Fielder's Sponge (below right)

FRUIT CAKE

675 g mixed fruit

¼ cup mixed peel

3 tablespoons Edmonds high grade flour

225 g butter

1 cup brown sugar

2 tablespoons golden syrup

1 tablespoon marmalade

3 cups Edmonds high grade flour

1 teaspoon Edmonds baking powder

pinch of salt

1 teaspoon mixed spice

½ teaspoon ground nutmeg

5 eggs, beaten

Combine mixed fruit and peel in a bowl. Dust with the first measure of flour. Cream butter, sugar and golden syrup until light and fluffy. Stir in marmalade. Sift the second measure of flour, baking powder, salt, mixed spice and nutmeg together. Add flour and eggs alternately to creamed mixture. Add prepared fruit and mix well. Line a deep, 20 cm square cake tin with two layers of brown paper followed by one layer of baking paper. Spoon mixture into cake tin, smoothing the surface. Bake at 150°C for 2–2½ hours or until an inserted skewer comes out clean. Leave in tin until cold.

LEMON CURD AND YOGHURT CAKE

250 g butter, softened
1½ cups caster sugar
4 eggs
finely grated zest of 1 lemon
2 cups Edmonds standard flour
2 teaspoons Edmonds
baking powder
½ cup lemon curd
(see recipe below)
¾ cup natural unsweetened
yoghurt

icing sugar to dust
citrus leaves to garnish
whipped cream to serve

LEMON CURD
50 g butter
¾ cup sugar
1 cup lemon juice
2 eggs, beaten
1 teaspoon finely grated
lemon zest

Cream butter and sugar until light and fluffy. Add eggs one at a time, beating well after each addition. Beat in lemon zest. Sift flour and baking powder together. Combine lemon curd and yoghurt. Fold dry ingredients into creamed mixture alternately with lemon curd mixture. Spoon into a deep 22 cm round cake tin that has been greased and lined with baking paper. Bake at 180°C for 50–55 minutes. Cool in tin. Dust with icing sugar and garnish with citrus leaves. Serve with cream. To make the Lemon Curd, melt the butter in the top of a double boiler. Stir in sugar and lemon juice until sugar is dissolved. Add eggs and lemon zest. Place over boiling water and cook, stirring all the time until mixture thickens. Cool. Store in the refrigerator in a covered container.

LEMON SEMOLINA CAKE

3 tablespoons Edmonds standard flour

¾ cup semolina

4 eggs

½ cup sugar

1 tablespoon grated lemon rind

SYRUP

1 cup sugar

½ cup water

¼ cup lemon juice

1 teaspoon grated lemon rind

In a bowl combine flour and semolina. Separate the eggs. Beat egg yolks and sugar together until pale and thick. Gently fold semolina mixture and lemon rind into egg mixture. Beat egg whites until peaks just fold over. Fold a quarter of egg whites into egg mixture, then remaining egg whites. Pour mixture into a 20 cm round springform tin lined on the base with baking paper. Bake at 180°C for 40 minutes or until a skewer inserted in centre of cake comes out clean. Leave in tin for 10 minutes before transferring to a serving plate. To make the syrup, place sugar, water, lemon juice and rind in a small saucepan. Heat gently, stirring constantly until sugar has dissolved. Pour hot syrup over cake about a quarter at a time, leaving time for the cake to soak up the syrup.

MACAROON CAKE

100 g butter

½ cup sugar

3 egg yolks

1½ cups Edmonds standard flour

2 teaspoons Edmonds baking powder

½ cup milk

1 teaspoon vanilla essence

½ cup raspberry jam

TOPPING

3 egg whites

¾ cup caster sugar

1½ cups coconut

1 teaspoon almond essence

Melt butter in a saucepan large enough to mix all the ingredients. Stir in sugar and egg yolks. Sift flour and baking powder into the saucepan. Add milk and vanilla essence and mix with a wooden spoon to combine. Spoon mixture into a 20 cm round springform tin lined on the base with baking paper. Spread jam over batter. Spread topping over jam. To make the topping, beat egg whites until stiff. Gradually beat in sugar and continue beating until mixture is thick. Mix in coconut and almond essence. Bake at 180°C for 45–50 minutes or until an inserted skewer comes out clean. Cool in tin for 10 minutes before releasing the sides of the tin.

MADEIRA CAKE

250 g butter, softened
1 cup sugar
½ teaspoon grated lemon rind
4 eggs
2¼ cups Edmonds standard flour
1½ teaspoons Edmonds baking powder

Cream butter and sugar until light and fluffy. Stir in lemon rind. In a separate bowl beat eggs until thick. Sift flour and baking powder together. Add to creamed mixture alternately with the eggs. Stir to mix. Spoon mixture into a 20 cm square cake tin lined on the base with baking paper. Bake at 180°C for 30 minutes or until the cake springs back when lightly touched. Leave in tin for 10 minutes before turning out onto a wire rack.

Moist Apple Walnut Cake (top left)
Madeira Cake (top right)
Marble Cake (bottom centre)

MARBLE CAKE

125 g butter, softened

1 cup sugar

2 eggs

1½ cups Edmonds standard flour

1½ teaspoons Edmonds baking powder

¼ cup milk

2 tablespoons cocoa

2 drops red food colouring

CHOCOLATE ICING (see page 112)

Cream butter and sugar until light and fluffy. Add eggs one at a time, beating well after each addition. Sift together flour and baking powder. Fold into creamed mixture alternately with milk. Divide mixture into three equal parts. Into one portion stir the cocoa, and to another the food colouring. Leave the last portion plain. Spoon stripes of the three mixtures into a greased and lined 20 cm round cake tin. Bake at 180°C for 50 minutes or until a skewer inserted in the centre of the cake comes out clean. Leave in tin for 10 minutes before turning out onto a wire rack. When cold, spread with Chocolate Icing.

MOIST APPLE WALNUT CAKE

4 eggs

2 cups sugar

1 cup vegetable oil

1 cup roughly chopped walnuts

2 cups grated unpeeled Granny Smith apple (2 medium apples)

440 g can unsweetened crushed pineapple, drained

2 cups Edmonds standard flour

1½ teaspoons Edmonds baking powder

¾ teaspoon Edmonds baking soda

2 teaspoons cinnamon

1 teaspoon mixed spice

CREAM CHEESE ICING (see page 112)

lemon zest to garnish

Using a wooden spoon beat together eggs, sugar and oil until sugar dissolves. Stir in walnuts, apple and pineapple. Combine flour, baking powder, soda and spices. Stir into egg mixture. Transfer to a greased deep 20 cm square cake tin that has had the base lined with baking paper. Bake at 180°C for 1¼ hours. Leave cake in tin for 15 minutes before transferring to a wire rack. When cold, spread with Cream Cheese Icing and garnish with lemon zest.

MUD CAKE

BASE

200 g packet chocolate
thin biscuits

75 g butter

½ cup chocolate
hazelnut spread

CAKE

50 g butter

1 cup sugar

3 eggs

1 tablespoon vanilla essence

1½ cups Edmonds standard
flour

3 teaspoons Edmonds I
baking powder

3 tablespoons cocoa

¼ cup boiling water

½ cup milk

icing sugar to dust

ready-made chocolate sauce

To make the base, crush biscuits into fine crumbs. Melt butter and mix into biscuit crumbs. Press over the base of a 20 cm round cake tin lined on the base with baking paper. Spread with hazelnut spread. To make the cake, melt butter in a saucepan large enough to mix all the ingredients. Remove from heat. Add sugar, eggs and vanilla. Sift flour and baking powder together. Mix cocoa into boiling water. Fold flour, cocoa mixture and milk into butter mixture. Pour over base. Bake at 180°C for 45–50 minutes, or until cake springs back when lightly touched. Cool in tin for 10 minutes before turning onto a wire rack. Dust with icing sugar and serve with chocolate sauce.

ORANGE POLENTA CAKE

125 g butter, softened

1 cup caster sugar

2 eggs

finely grated zest of 1 orange

¼ cup freshly squeezed orange juice

¼ cup orange marmalade

1 cup Edmonds standard flour

1 teaspoon Edmonds baking powder

½ cup polenta

70 g packet ground almonds

½ cup milk

orange zest to garnish

Cream butter and sugar until light and fluffy. Add eggs one at a time, beating well after each addition. Beat in orange rind, juice and marmalade. Sift flour and baking powder together. Fold flour, polenta, almonds and milk into creamed mixture. Spoon into a 20 cm round cake tin that has been greased and lined with baking paper. Bake at 180°C for 45 minutes or until a skewer inserted in the centre of the cake comes out clean. Leave cake in tin for 10 minutes before turning onto a wire rack. Garnish with orange zest.

PANFORTE

1 cup hazelnuts, toasted, shelled and roughly chopped
1 cup blanched almonds, toasted and roughly chopped
½ cup dried figs, chopped
½ cup dried apricots, chopped
¼ cup crystallised ginger, chopped
¼ cup mixed peel
¾ cup Edmonds high grade flour
1 teaspoon cinnamon
¾ teaspoon ground nutmeg
¼ teaspoon ground cloves
½ cup runny honey
½ cup caster sugar

Thoroughly grease a 20 cm round cake tin. Line the base and sides with baking paper. Combine nuts, dried fruit, flour and spices in a mixing bowl. Mix well. Place honey and sugar in a small saucepan. Stir over a low heat until sugar dissolves. Bring to the boil, stirring constantly. Boil for about 2 minutes until mixture reaches the "soft ball" stage. To test for soft ball stage, drop a small amount of mixture off a teaspoon into cold water. When a soft ball forms, the mixture is ready. On a sugar thermometer, the soft ball stage is 116°C. Do not let the syrup change colour. Remove from the heat and let the bubbles subside. Carefully pour syrup over dry ingredients, then quickly mix to combine. Press into prepared tin. (Speed is vital, as the mixture will become sticky and unmanageable very quickly.) Bake at 150°C for 45 minutes in the lower third of the oven. Cool in tin. Wrap in foil and store in the refrigerator. To serve, cut into thin wedges.

RICH CHOCOLATE CAKE

(A VERY MOIST AND RICH FLOURLESS CAKE. SUITABLE FOR DESSERT.)

175 g unsalted butter, softened

¾ cup brown sugar

1 teaspoon vanilla essence

6 eggs, separated

150 g dark cooking chocolate, melted

2 x 70 g packets ground almonds

icing sugar

whipped cream

Cream butter, sugar and vanilla until light and fluffy. Beat in egg yolks. Fold in melted chocolate and almonds. In another bowl beat egg whites until soft peaks form. Gradually fold whites into chocolate mixture. Pour into a greased and lined 20 cm springform tin. Bake at 190°C for 20 minutes then reduce heat to 150°C for a further 35 minutes or until firm. Allow cake to cool in tin. Release cake and transfer to a serving plate. Dust with icing sugar and serve warm or cold with cream.

CHOCOLATE LIQUEUR CAKE

Omit vanilla essence and replace with 2 teaspoons chocolate, coffee or orange liqueur.

Sultana Cake (top left)
Rich Chocolate Cake (below left)
Tosca Cake (below right)

SULTANA CAKE

2 cups sultanas
250 g butter, chopped in small pieces
2 cups sugar
3 eggs, beaten
½ teaspoon lemon or almond essence
3 cups Edmonds standard flour
1½ teaspoons Edmonds baking powder

Put sultanas in a saucepan. Cover with water. Bring to the boil then simmer for 15 minutes. Drain thoroughly. Add butter. In a bowl beat sugar into eggs until well combined. Add sultana mixture and essence. Sift flour and baking powder together. Mix sifted ingredients into fruit mixture. Spoon mixture into a greased and lined 20 cm square cake tin. Bake at 160°C for 1–1½ hours or until cake springs back when lightly touched. Leave in tin for 10 minutes before turning onto a wire rack.

TOSCA CAKE

2 eggs

½ cup sugar

¾ cup Edmonds standard flour

1 teaspoon Edmonds baking powder

75 g butter, melted

2 tablespoons milk

TOPPING

3 tablespoons melted butter

70 g packet slivered almonds

¼ cup sugar

2 tablespoons milk

Beat eggs and sugar until pale and thick. Sift flour and baking powder together. Carefully fold into egg mixture. Fold in melted butter and milk. Pour into a greased 25 cm loose-bottomed flan tin. Bake at 180°C for about 30 minutes or until cake springs back when lightly touched. Remove from oven and quickly spoon topping over. To make the topping, heat butter, almonds and sugar in a saucepan. Stir constantly until sugar has dissolved. Add milk and bring to the boil. Reduce heat and simmer for 5 minutes, stirring occasionally. Return cake to oven and bake for about 10 minutes or until topping is golden and caramelised. Leave in tin for 10 minutes before turning out onto a wire rack.

WARM GINGERBREAD DATE CAKE

1 cup pitted dates, roughly chopped

1½ cups water

¾ teaspoon Edmonds baking soda

2 eggs

¾ cup brown sugar

½ cup vegetable oil

¼ cup golden syrup

¼ cup chopped crystallised ginger

2½ cups Edmonds standard flour

2 tablespoons cocoa

1 teaspoon Edmonds baking powder

2 teaspoons ground ginger

icing sugar to dust

whipped cream to serve

Combine dates and water in a small saucepan. Bring to the boil. Remove from heat and stir in baking soda. Cool for 10 minutes. In a large bowl, whisk together eggs, sugar, oil, golden syrup and crystallised ginger. Sift together flour, cocoa, baking powder and ground ginger. Stir date mixture into egg mixture. Lastly, fold in dry ingredients. Spoon into a greased and paper lined 22 cm round cake tin. Bake at 180°C for 50–55 minutes or until a skewer inserted in the centre of the cake comes out clean. Stand for 10 minutes before turning onto a wire rack. Serve warm or cold, dusted with icing sugar and accompanied by cream.

FILLINGS AND ICINGS

CREAM CHEESE ICING
2 tablespoons butter, softened
¼ cup cream cheese
1 cup icing sugar
½ teaspoon grated lemon rind

Beat butter and cream cheese until creamy. Mix in icing sugar and lemon rind, beating well to combine.

WHITE ICING
2 cups icing sugar
¼ teaspoon butter, softened
2 tablespoons water, approximately
½ teaspoon vanilla essence

Sift icing sugar into a bowl. Add butter. Add sufficient water to mix to a spreadable consistency. Flavour with vanilla essence.

CHOCOLATE ICING
Sift 1 tablespoon cocoa with the icing sugar.

COFFEE ICING
Dissolve 2 teaspoons instant coffee in 1 tablespoon hot water. Mix into icing sugar.

LEMON ICING
Replace vanilla with 1 teaspoon grated lemon rind. Replace water with lemon juice. Add a few drops of yellow food colouring if wished.

PIES, PIZZAS, BREADS *and* BUNS

BASIC PIZZA

PIZZA DOUGH

1 tablespoon Edmonds active yeast

½ teaspoon sugar

1 cup tepid water

1 teaspoon salt

3 cups Edmonds standard flour

1 tablespoon oil

Combine yeast, sugar and water in a bowl. Set aside for 15 minutes or until frothy. Combine salt and flour in a large bowl. Add yeast mixture and oil. Mix to a soft dough. Transfer to a lightly floured surface and knead for 5 minutes, until smooth and elastic. Place dough in a lightly oiled large bowl and cover with a tea-towel. Stand in a warm place until doubled in bulk. Punch dough down in the centre, knead lightly for 1 minute and roll into a 30 cm circle. Place on a lightly greased oven tray. Top with ingredients of your choice. Cook at 220°C for 15 minutes or until well risen and golden. Serves 4.
N.B. To cook pizza on a pizza stone, transfer completed uncooked pizza to a heated pizza stone and cook as above.

TOMATO SAUCE

1 tablespoon oil

1 onion, finely chopped

1 teaspoon crushed garlic

400 g can tomatoes in juice

2 tablespoons tomato paste

1 tablespoon chopped basil

salt and freshly ground black pepper

Heat oil in a frying pan. Cook onion for 5 minutes until soft. Add garlic, tomatoes and tomato paste, breaking up the tomatoes with a wooden spoon. Simmer for about 20 minutes until sauce is thick. Stir in basil. Season to taste.

PIZZA TOPPING COMBINATIONS

VEGETARIAN PIZZA
Spread the prepared pizza base with herb pesto. Top with roasted sliced eggplant, thinly sliced red onion, crumbled feta cheese, sliced cherry tomatoes and a scattering of grated mozzarella cheese.

GREEK PIZZA
Spread the prepared pizza base with Tomato Sauce (see page 117). Top with diced feta cheese, pitted halved olives, thinly sliced red onion, strips of roasted red capsicum and grated mozzarella cheese.

CHICKEN AND BLUE CHEESE PIZZA
Spread the prepared pizza base with herb pesto. Top with a little grated cheddar cheese, shredded cooked chicken, crumbled blue cheese, chopped walnuts and halved cherry tomatoes.

PIZZA SUPREME

Spread the prepared pizza base with Tomato Sauce (see page 117). Top with sliced salami, diced ham, anchovies, strips of roasted red capsicum, halved button mushrooms, pitted halved olives, thinly sliced red onion and grated mozzarella cheese.

BARBECUE PIZZA

Spread the prepared pizza base with a barbecue-style sauce. Top with sliced cooked chicken, onion rings, chopped coriander, grated cheddar or mozzarella cheese and a sprinkling of grated parmesan cheese.

SALAMI, TOMATO AND CAPER PIZZA

Spread the prepared pizza base with Tomato Sauce (see page 117). Top with sliced salami, sliced tomatoes, capers and grated mozzarella cheese.

RAJAH'S PIZZA

PIZZA BASE

½ teaspoon sugar

½ cup tepid water

2 teaspoons Edmonds
active yeast

1–1¼ cups Edmonds high
grade flour

½ teaspoon salt

1 tablespoon olive oil

TOPPING

250 g chicken tenderloins

2 teaspoons oil

½ cup fruit chutney

YOGHURT DIP

½ cup natural unsweetened
yoghurt

½ cup chopped cucumber

1 tablespoon chopped coriander
or parsley

To make the dough, dissolve sugar in water. Sprinkle over yeast and leave for 10 minutes or until frothy. Place 1 cup of flour and salt in a bowl. Mix in yeast mixture and olive oil to form a stiff dough. Add more flour if necessary. Knead dough until smooth and elastic. Place in a greased bowl. Turn dough over and cover with plastic wrap. Set aside in a warm place until double in bulk. Slice chicken tenderloins in half lengthways. Heat oil in a frying pan. Cook chicken for 6–8 minutes until golden and cooked through. Punch dough down and knead until smooth. Shape and flatten into a 30 cm round. Place on a baking tray. Spread with chutney to within 1 cm of edge of dough. Arrange chicken on top. Bake at 200°C for 15 minutes or until cooked. Combine yoghurt, cucumber and parsley. Serve in a small bowl to accompany pizza. Serves 3–4.

DEEP PAN PIZZA

1 quantity Pizza Dough
(see page 117)
olive oil to brush

FILLING
1 tablespoon oil
300 g lean beef mince
1 onion, finely chopped
1 teaspoon crushed garlic
400 g can tomatoes in juice
2 tablespoons tomato paste

salt and freshly ground black
pepper to season
1 red capsicum, sliced
1 green or yellow capsicum, sliced
6 mushrooms, sliced
½ cup pitted black
olives, halved
¼ cup chopped sundried tomatoes
1 cup grated tasty cheddar cheese
¼ cup freshly grated
parmesan cheese

Roll out the risen dough on a lightly floured surface to a size to fit the base and halfway up the sides of a 22-cm-round springform tin. Brush the tin with oil and transfer the dough to the tin. To make the filling, heat the oil in a frying pan. Cook the mince and onion for 5 minutes until the mince has browned. Add the garlic, tomatoes in juice and tomato paste, breaking up the tomatoes with a wooden spoon. Cook for 25 minutes until the mixture is thick. Season. Cool. Spoon the mince mixture into prepared base. Arrange the capsicums, mushrooms, olives and sundried tomatoes on top of the mince. Sprinkle over cheeses. Bake at 200°C for 30 minutes until golden. Stand for 5 minutes before releasing from the sides of the tin and slicing into wedges.

Parmesan and Garlic Twists (Top left)
Deep Pan Pizza (Bottom left)
Feta, Olive and Sundried Tomato Calzone (Right)

PARMESAN AND GARLIC TWISTS

DOUGH

1½ teaspoons sugar

300 ml warm water

1 tablespoon Edmonds
active yeast

3 cups Edmonds high grade flour

1½ teaspoons salt

2 tablespoons olive oil

TOPPING

2 tablespoons olive oil

1 clove garlic, crushed

2–3 tablespoons freshly grated
parmesan cheese

1 tablespoon finely
chopped rosemary

rock salt to sprinkle (optional)

Dissolve the sugar in warm water. Sprinkle the yeast over the water and set aside in a warm place for 10 minutes until frothy. Combine the flour and salt in a large bowl. Stir in frothy yeast mixture and oil. Mix to a soft dough. Transfer the dough to a liberally floured surface and knead for 5 minutes until smooth and elastic. Divide the dough into 8 equal portions. To make each twist, take a portion of the dough and divide in half. Roll each piece into a 20-cm-long sausage shape. Twist the dough lengths together by using a dab of olive oil at the join and squeezing the dough ends to secure. Place the twists on a lightly greased oven tray, allowing room for spreading. To make the topping, combine oil and garlic. Brush the twists with the oil mixture. Cover with plastic wrap and sit in a warm place for about 45 minutes until well risen. Sprinkle with parmesan cheese, rosemary and rock salt. Bake at 220°C for 10 minutes, then reduce temperature to 200°C and bake for a further 5 minutes until golden.

Makes 8 twists.

FETA, OLIVE AND SUNDRIED TOMATO CALZONE

DOUGH
1½ teaspoons sugar
300 ml warm water
2 tablespoons Edmonds
active yeast
3 cups Edmonds high grade flour
1½ teaspoons salt
¼ cup olive oil

FILLING
75 g olive tapenade

100 g feta cheese, cut into 1 cm dice
2 roasted capsicums, peeled,
seeded and sliced
4 artichoke hearts, sliced
¼ cup chopped
sundried tomatoes
½ cup grated mozzarella cheese

olive oil to brush
¼ cup freshly grated
parmesan cheese

Dissolve the sugar in the warm water. Sprinkle the yeast over the water and set aside in a warm place for 10 minutes until frothy. Combine the flour and salt in a large bowl. Stir in the frothy yeast mixture and oil. Mix to a soft dough. Transfer the dough to a liberally floured surface and knead for 5 minutes until smooth and elastic. Place the dough in an oiled bowl. Turn the dough to coat with oil. Cover with plastic wrap and stand in a warm place for 45 minutes until the dough is well risen. Divide the dough into 4 equal portions. Roll each portion into a 20 cm circle. Cover half of each circle with filling ingredients to within 1 cm of the edge of the dough. First, spread with the tapenade, then with layers of feta, capsicums, artichokes, sundried tomatoes and mozzarella. Lightly brush the edge of the dough with water. Fold the unfilled portion of dough over the filling and crimp edges together to seal. Transfer the calzone to a lightly greased baking tray. Brush lightly with oil. Sprinkle with parmesan. Bake at 220°C for 10 minutes, then reduce the temperature to 200°C and bake for a further 10–15 minutes until golden.

FISH PIE

6 large potatoes, peeled and cooked

25 g butter

1 tablespoon milk

salt and freshly ground black pepper

2 tablespoons butter

2 tablespoons Edmonds standard flour

1 cup milk

500 g smoked fish, flaked, or 425 g can tuna, drained and flaked

1 tablespoon chopped parsley

2 hard-boiled eggs, chopped

Mash potatoes with butter and milk. Season to taste with salt and pepper. Line a 20 cm pie dish with half the potatoes. Set remaining potatoes aside. Heat second measure of butter in a saucepan. Add flour and stir constantly for 2 minutes. Remove pan from heat. Gradually add second measure of milk, stirring constantly. Return pan to heat, stirring continuously until sauce boils and thickens. Remove from heat. Add fish, parsley and eggs. Pour mixture into the lined pie dish. Cover with remaining potato. Cook at 190°C for 20 minutes or until golden.
Serves 4.

LATTICE PIE

2 tablespoons butter

1 small onion, chopped

½ teaspoon curry powder

2 tablespoons Edmonds standard flour

¾ cup milk

310 g can smoked fish, drained and flaked

freshly ground black pepper

2 sheets pre-rolled flaky pastry

1 egg yolk

1 tablespoon water

Melt butter in a saucepan. Add onion and cook until clear. Stir in curry powder. Cook for 30 seconds. Stir in flour and cook for 2 minutes. Remove pan from heat. Gradually add milk, stirring constantly. Return pan to heat, stirring constantly until mixture boils and thickens. Remove from heat. Lightly mix in fish. Season to taste with pepper. Cool. Place a sheet of pastry on oven tray. Spread fish mixture over pastry, leaving a 2 cm edge all the way round. Dampen this edge lightly with water. Carefully fold second sheet of pastry in half. From centre fold make 1.5-cm-wide cuts to within 2 cm of edge. Open pastry out and carefully lift over filling. Press edges firmly together. Whisk together egg yolk and water. Brush top surface of pastry with this mixture, making sure egg does not drip down sides as this will prevent pastry from rising. Cook at 220°C for 20 minutes or until golden and well risen. Serve with a tossed salad.
Serves 4–6.

SHEPHERD'S PIE

1 tablespoon oil

1 onion, chopped

500 g lean beef mince

2 tablespoons Edmonds standard flour

1 tablespoon tomato sauce

1 tablespoon chutney or relish

1 tablespoon Worcestershire sauce

¾ cup liquid beef stock

salt and freshly ground black pepper to season

4 potatoes, peeled and chopped

1 tablespoon butter

1 cup grated tasty cheese

Heat oil in a large frying pan. Add onion and cook for 5 minutes until soft. Add mince and cook until well browned, stirring constantly. Stir in flour and cook for 1 minute. Add tomato sauce, chutney, Worcestershire sauce and stock. Bring to the boil, reduce heat and simmer for 5 minutes. Season to taste. Set aside. Cook potatoes in boiling, lightly salted water until tender. Drain and heat for a few minutes to dry off excess moisture. Shake the pan frequently during this time. Mash potato and butter. Add half the cheese, mixing until smooth and creamy. Season with salt and pepper to taste. Put mince into a pie dish. Top with potato mixture. Sprinkle with remaining cheese. Bake at 190°C for 25–30 minutes or until golden and heated through. Serves 3–4.

Shepherd's Pie (Top)
Steak and Kidney Pie (Bottom left)
Family Chicken Pie (Bottom right)

STEAK AND KIDNEY PIE

500 g beef chuck or blade steak
150 g beef or lamb kidneys
2 tablespoons oil
1 onion, chopped
2 stalks celery, sliced
1 tablespoon Edmonds standard flour
1 cup liquid beef stock

¼ cup tomato puree
½ teaspoon mixed herbs
salt and freshly ground black pepper
200 g flaky pastry
1 egg yolk
1 tablespoon water

Trim fat from meat and cut into 2 cm cubes. Heat oil in a heavy-based frying pan. Add meat in batches and quickly brown on all sides. Using a slotted spoon, remove meat from pan and set aside. Add onion and celery and cook for 5 minutes until onion is soft. Stir in flour and cook for 30 seconds. Remove pan from heat. Gradually add stock, stirring constantly. Return pan to heat, stirring constantly until mixture comes to the boil. Return meat to pan. Stir in tomato puree and herbs. Cover and cook gently for 1 hour or until meat is tender. Season with salt and pepper to taste. Using a slotted spoon, transfer meat and vegetables to a 20 cm pie plate or dish. Pour ¼ cup of the cooking liquid over the meat. Reserve remaining liquid. Allow to cool. On a lightly floured board roll out pastry to 3 cm larger than the pie plate or dish. Cut a 3 cm wide strip off the edge. Wet edge of pie plate with water and place the pastry strip all round. Cover with pastry round, pressing edges firmly together. Pierce holes in centre of pie. Decorate with any pastry trimmings. Beat egg yolk and water together. Brush over pastry. Bake at 220°C for 20 minutes or until golden and well risen. Reheat reserved cooking liquid and serve with the pie. Serves 4.

FAMILY CHICKEN PIE

8 boneless chicken thighs

2 tablespoons oil

3 rashers bacon, chopped

100 g button mushrooms, halved

1 onion, chopped

1 clove garlic, crushed

3 tablespoons Edmonds
standard flour

1 cup liquid chicken stock

¼ teaspoon mixed herbs

½ cup milk

½ teaspoon salt

white pepper

1 cup drained canned
corn kernels

200 g flaky pastry

1 egg yolk

Remove skin from chicken. Cut flesh into 2.5 cm cubes. Heat oil in a large saucepan. Add bacon, mushrooms, onion and garlic. Cook for 5 minutes until onion is soft. Stir in flour and cook for 1 minute. Remove pan from heat. Gradually add stock, stirring constantly. Return pan to heat stirring constantly until mixture comes to the boil. Add chicken, herbs, milk, salt and pepper to taste. Reduce heat and cook gently for 20 minutes or until juices run clear when tested, stirring occasionally. Remove from heat and allow to cool. Stir in corn. Pour chicken mixture into a 20 cm pie dish. Alternatively, divide between 6 individual pie dishes. Brush edge of dish with water. On a lightly floured surface roll out pastry to a circle large enough to fit top of pie dish. Carefully place pastry over filling. Press edges firmly to seal, then trim. Decorate pie with pastry trimmings. Cut steam holes in centre of pastry top. Brush pastry with egg yolk. Bake at 220°C for 20 minutes or until pastry is golden and well risen.
Serves 6.

CHICKEN AND APRICOT FILO PARCELS

1 teaspoon oil

1 small onion, finely chopped

1 tablespoon grated root ginger

1 cup chopped dried apricots

¼ cup orange juice

4 single skinless, boneless chicken breasts

8 sheets filo pastry

1½ cups fresh breadcrumbs

¼ cup melted butter

1 tablespoon sesame seeds

Heat oil in a saucepan and sauté onion and ginger for 5 minutes or until onion is clear. Add apricots and orange juice. Simmer for 5 minutes or until pulpy. Cool. Remove skin from chicken and cut a long pocket in the side of each breast. Fill with apricot mixture. Cut filo pastry sheets crossways. Keep pastry under a damp tea-towel until ready to work with it. Sprinkle breadcrumbs between 4 squares of pastry. Place chicken breast on top of the pastry layer. Fold pastry over chicken to make a neat parcel. Place seam side down on a greased oven tray. Brush with melted butter and sprinkle with sesame seeds. Bake at 190°C for 20 minutes or until golden and cooked. Serve with a tossed salad.

Serves 4.

PUMPKIN AND CHICKEN FILO PIES

2 cups (275 g) peeled, seeded and diced pumpkin

1 large potato, peeled and diced

1 tablespoon butter to mash

2 tablespoons oil

2 onions, finely chopped

2 teaspoons ground cumin

1 teaspoon garam masala

1 single boneless, skinless chicken breast, diced

1 teaspoon crushed garlic

1 cup grated tasty cheddar cheese

salt and freshly ground black pepper to season

50 g butter, melted

18 sheets filo pastry

Cook the pumpkin and potato until tender. Drain. Add the butter and mash. Heat the oil in a frying pan and cook onion, cumin, garam masala and chicken for 6–8 minutes until onion is soft. Add the garlic and cook for 2 minutes. Combine mashed vegetable mixture, chicken mixture and cheese. Season. Brush 12 deep muffin tins with melted butter. For each pie, lightly brush a sheet of filo pastry with melted butter. Fold in half widthways, then brush with butter. Fold in half again. Line prepared tins with the pastry. Spoon the filling into pastry shells. Cut the remaining 6 sheets of filo pastry in half widthways. Scrunch each portion into a ball and place on top of pies, Brush with melted butter. Bake at 190°C for 20 minutes until golden. Stand for 8–10 minutes before serving.

Makes 12 pies.

RUSTIC BEEF AND VEGETABLE PASTIES

FILLING

1 tablespoon oil

1 onion, finely diced

500 g lean beef or lamb mince

2 cloves garlic, crushed

2 teaspoons curry powder

1 potato, peeled and finely diced

1 carrot, peeled and finely diced

1 cup peeled, seeded and
finely diced pumpkin

410 g can tomato puree

1 cup water

salt and freshly ground black
pepper to season

PASTRY

300 ml cold water

200 g butter, chopped

2 teaspoons salt

4 cups Edmonds standard flour

4 teaspoons Edmonds baking powder

1 egg, beaten

To make filling, heat oil in a frying pan. Cook onion and mince until meat has browned. Add garlic and curry powder and stir for 1–2 minutes. Add vegetables, tomato puree and water. Cover and simmer for 10 minutes. Remove lid and cook for a further 30 minutes until vegetables are cooked and sauce is thick. Season to taste. Cool. To make pastry, combine water, butter and salt in a saucepan. Stir over a medium heat until butter melts. Remove from heat. Add flour and baking powder and stir quickly until it forms a ball. Transfer to a floured surface and cool for 5 minutes. Knead dough for 1 minute. While dough is warm, divide into 12 equal portions. Cover with foil to keep warm. Roll each portion into a 16 cm circle. Brush with beaten egg. Spread one-twelfth of the meat mixture over half the circle, leaving a 1.5 cm pastry border. Fold pastry over filling to enclose. Crimp edges together with fingertips. Transfer to a greased baking tray. Brush pasties all over with egg. Bake at 190°C for 30 minutes until golden. Makes 12 pasties.

CURRIED VEGETABLE PARCELS

2 tablespoons oil

2 cups small cauliflower florets

2 cups peeled, seeded and finely diced pumpkin

1 onion, chopped

1 courgette, thinly sliced

1 red capsicum, seeded and sliced

1 green capsicum, seeded and sliced

1 tablespoon curry powder

1 teaspoon crushed garlic

6 tablespoons coconut milk powder

½ cup warm water

18 sheets filo pastry

50 g butter, melted

relish or chutney to serve

Heat the oil in a heavy-based frying pan. Cook all the vegetables and the curry powder for 5 minutes over a low-medium heat, stirring frequently. Cover the pan and cook for about 10 minutes, stirring occasionally, until the vegetables are tender. Add the garlic. Mix the coconut milk powder and water to a smooth paste. Add to the pan, stirring well. Simmer, uncovered, for 6–8 minutes or until the sauce is thick. Cool. For each parcel, lay a sheet of filo pastry on a flat surface. Brush with melted butter. Layer 2 more sheets of the pastry on top, brushing between each sheet with butter. Fold pastry in half widthways. Spoon one-sixth of the vegetable mixture in a line (about 8 cm long) along one long edge of the pastry. Roll up to form a log. Squeeze the pastry together around each end of the filling to form a cracker. Place the parcels on a greased baking tray. Brush with melted butter. Bake at 190°C for 12–15 minutes until golden. Serve immediately accompanied by relish or chutney. Makes 6 parcels.

BASIC QUICHE

SHORT PASTRY
1 cup Edmonds standard flour

¼ teaspoon salt

60 g butter

2–3 tablespoons cold water

FILLING
1 tablespoon butter

3 rashers bacon, chopped

1 onion, chopped

2 tablespoons Edmonds standard flour

1 cup milk

2 eggs, lightly beaten

½ cup grated tasty cheese

salt and freshly ground black pepper to season

To make the pastry, sift together flour and salt. Cut in butter until it resembles fine breadcrumbs. Add sufficient water to mix to a stiff dough. Roll pastry out on a lightly floured surface to fit a 20 cm flan ring or quiche dish, handling the pastry as little as possible. If using flan ring, place ring on an oven tray before lining with pastry. Trim excess pastry off and discard. Bake blind at 200°C for 12 minutes. (To bake blind, cut a circle of baking paper to cover pastry. Fill with dried beans or rice.) Remove baking blind material. Return to the oven for 1 minute to dry pastry out. Remove from oven. Pour filling into pastry base. To make the filling, melt butter in a saucepan. Cook bacon and onion for 5 minutes until onion is clear. Add flour, stirring constantly for 2 minutes. Remove pan from heat. Gradually add milk, stirring constantly. Return pan to heat, stirring continuously until sauce thickens and boils. Remove pan from heat. Add eggs and cheese to sauce. Stir to combine. Season. Bake quiche for 30 minutes or until filling is golden and set. Serve hot or cold.
Serves 4–6.

APPLE PIE

SWEET SHORTCRUST PASTRY
(makes 200 g)
1 cup Edmonds standard flour
75 g butter
¼ cup sugar
1 egg yolk
1 tablespoon water

FILLING
4–6 Granny Smith apples
½ cup sugar
25 g butter, melted
2 tablespoons Edmonds
standard flour
¼ teaspoon ground cloves

2 teaspoons sugar to sprinkle

To make pastry, sift flour. Cut butter into flour until it resembles fine breadcrumbs. Stir in first measure of sugar. Add yolk and water. Mix to a stiff dough. Cover with plastic wrap and chill for 30 minutes before using. On a lightly floured surface, roll out pastry slightly larger than a 20 cm pie plate. Cut two 2.5-cm-wide strips long enough to go around the edge of the pie plate. Brush with water. Spoon apple filling into centre of pie plate. To make the filling, peel, core and slice apples thinly. Combine sugar, butter, flour and cloves. Toss apples in this mixture. Cover with remaining pastry. Press edges firmly together to seal. Cut steam holes in centre of pastry. Trim and crimp edges. Decorate pie with any pastry trimmings. Brush lightly with milk or water. Sprinkle with sugar. Bake at 200°C for 25 minutes or until pastry is golden. Test with a skewer if the apple is cooked. If not, reduce oven temperature to 180°C and cook until apple is tender.
Serves 6.

Fruit Tartlets (Top)
Apple Pie (Bottom left)
Neenish Tarts (Bottom right)

FRUIT TARTLETS

SWEET SHORTCRUST PASTRY

(makes 200 g)

1 cup Edmonds standard flour

75 g butter

¼ cup sugar

1 egg yolk

1 tablespoon water

FILLING

3 tablespoons Edmonds custard powder

1 cup milk

2 egg yolks

2 tablespoons sugar

2 tablespoons brandy

½ cup cream, whipped

TOPPING

fresh or tinned fruit – e.g. kiwifruit, grapes, strawberries, melon, diced or sliced

GLAZE

¼ cup apricot jam

2 teaspoons water

To make pastry, sift flour. Cut butter into flour until it resembles fine breadcrumbs. Stir in first measure of sugar. Add yolk and water. Mix to a stiff dough. Cover with plastic wrap and chill for 30 minutes before using. Roll the pastry out on a lightly floured surface to a thickness of 4 mm. Using a 7-cm-round fluted biscuit cutter, stamp circles from the dough. Line 18 x 7-cm-round tartlet tins. Prick the bases of pastry cases. Refrigerate for 10 minutes, then freeze for 5 minutes. Bake at 180°C for 12–15 minutes until golden. Cool. To make filling, mix custard powder to a smooth paste with a little of the milk. Whisk in remaining milk, yolks and sugar. Cook over a low heat, stirring constantly until the mixture thickens. Do not allow to boil. Stir in the brandy. Cover the surface of filling directly with plastic wrap. Cool for 1 hour. Fold in cream. Spoon filling into the prepared tartlet cases. Arrange the fruit on top of the custard. To make the glaze, gently heat together jam and water. Sieve. Spoon or brush glaze over the fruit.

Makes 18 tartlets.

NEENISH TARTS

PASTRY
125 g butter, softened
½ cup sugar
1 egg
2 cups Edmonds standard flour
1 teaspoon Edmonds baking powder
pinch of salt

FILLING
½ cup icing sugar
100 g butter, softened
½ cup sweetened condensed milk
2 tablespoons lemon juice

WHITE ICING
1 cup icing sugar
¼ teaspoon butter, softened
1 tablespoon water,
approximately
2 drops vanilla essence

CHOCOLATE ICING
as for White Icing, but add 2
teaspoons cocoa

To make the pastry, cream butter and sugar until light and fluffy. Add egg and beat well. Sift flour, baking powder and salt together. Mix into creamed mixture, stirring well. Turn mixture onto a lightly floured surface and knead well. Cover pastry and chill for 15 minutes. Roll out pastry to a 2 mm thickness. Cut out rounds using a 7-cm-round biscuit cutter and line pattytins. Prick bases. Refrigerate for 10 minutes then freeze for 5 minutes. Bake at 180°C for 12 minutes or until cooked. Cool pastry cases then fill with filling. To make the filling, sift icing sugar into a bowl. Add butter, condensed milk and lemon juice. Beat until smooth. Allow filling to set in the fridge. Ice one half of each tart with White Icing and the other half with Chocolate Icing. To make the icings, sift icing sugar into a bowl. Add butter, then sufficient water to mix to a spreadable consistency. Add essence. For the Chocolate Icing, sift the cocoa with the icing sugar.
Makes 24.

LEMON MERINGUE PIE

SWEET SHORTCBUST PASTRY
(makes 200 g)
1 cup Edmonds standard flour
75 g butter
¼ cup sugar
1 egg yolk
1 tablespoon water

FILLING
5 tablespoons Edmonds
Fielder's cornflour

1 cup sugar
2 teaspoons grated lemon zest
½ cup lemon juice
¾ cup water
4 eggs, separated
1 tablespoon butter

TOPPING
¼cup caster sugar
¼teaspoon vanilla essence

To make pastry, sift flour. Cut butter into flour until it resembles fine breadcrumbs. Stir in first measure of sugar. Add yolk and water. Mix to a stiff dough. Cover with plastic wrap and chill for 30 minutes before using. On a lightly floured surface roll out pastry to a 6 mm thickness. Use to line a 20 cm flan ring. Trim off any excess pastry. Bake blind at 190°C for 20 minutes. To bake blind, cut a circle of baking paper to cover the pastry. Fill with dried beans or rice.) Remove baking blind material. Return pastry shell to oven for 1 minute to dry out pastry base. While pastry is cooking make the filling. Blend cornflour, sugar, lemon zest and juice together until smooth. Add water. Cook over a medium heat until mixture boils and thickens, stirring constantly. Remove from heat. Stir in yolks and butter. Pour filling into cooked pastry base. Spoon meringue topping over lemon filling. To make the meringue, beat egg whites until stiff but not dry. Beat in sugar, 1 tablespoon at a time, until very thick and glossy. Stir in vanilla. Return to oven and bake at 190°C for 10 minutes or until golden.
Serves 6.

PECAN PIE

SWEET SHORTCRUST PASTRY	FILLING
(makes 200 g)	**100 g butter, softened**
1 cup Edmonds standard flour	**½ cup brown sugar**
75 g butter	**3 eggs**
¼ cup sugar	**¼ cup golden syrup**
1 egg yolk	**200 g pecan nuts**
1 tablespoon water	**1 tablespoon Edmonds standard flour**

To make pastry, sift flour. Cut butter into flour until it resembles fine breadcrumbs. Stir in first measure of sugar. Add yolk and water. Mix to a stiff dough. Cover with plastic wrap and chill for 30 minutes before using. On a lightly floured surface roll out pastry and use to line a 22 cm flan tin. Bake blind at 190°C for 15 minutes. (To bake blind, cut a circle of baking paper to cover the pastry. Fill with dried beans or rice.) Remove baking blind material. Return pastry shell to oven for 1 minute to dry out pastry base. Reduce oven temperature to 180°C. While the base is cooking, prepare the filling. Cream butter and sugar until light and fluffy. Add eggs one at a time, beating well after each addition. Beat in golden syrup. Toss pecans in flour, then stir into butter mixture. Pour into cooked pastry base. Return to oven and bake for a further 30 minutes or until filling is set.
Serves 6.

Chocolate Mud Pie (Top)
Pecan Pie (Bottom left)
Spiced Pumpkin Pie (Bottom right)

CHOCOLATE MUD PIE

PASTRY
1¼ cups Edmonds standard flour

¼ cup icing sugar

100 g butter, chopped

1 egg yolk

1–2 tablespoons cold water

FILLING
200 g butter, chopped

250 g dark chocolate, chopped

1½ cups sugar

½ cup water

1½ cups Edmonds standard flour

1 teaspoon Edmonds baking powder

½ cup cocoa

3 eggs

icing sugar to dust

whipped cream to serve

To make pastry, place flour, icing sugar and butter in a food processor. Pulse to the consistency of coarse crumbs. Add yolk and sufficient water to mix to a stiff dough. Wrap pastry in plastic wrap and refrigerate for 30 minutes. Roll out pastry on a lightly floured surface to fit a 26-cm-round, 3.5-cm-deep flan tin. Transfer to tin. Trim off any excess. Refrigerate for 10 minutes, then freeze for 5 minutes. Bake blind at 190°C for 12 minutes. (To bake blind, cut a circle of baking paper to cover the pastry. Fill with dried beans or rice.) Remove baking blind material and return to oven for 1 minute to dry out base. Reduce oven temperature to 160°C. While base is cooking, prepare filling. Place butter, chocolate, sugar and water in a medium saucepan. Stir over a low heat until butter and chocolate have melted. Remove from heat. Sift flour, baking powder and cocoa. Make a well in centre of dry ingredients. Add chocolate mixture and eggs, mixing until ingredients are just combined — do not overmix. Pour into prepared pastry shell. Bake for 1 hour until filling is set. Cool in tin. If desired, dust pie with icing sugar, using a template to transfer a pattern of your choice onto pie. Serve at room temperature in thin wedges. Accompany with whipped cream.

SPICED PUMPKIN PIE

PASTRY
1¼ cups Edmonds standard flour
¼ cup icing sugar
100 g cold butter, chopped
1 egg yolk
1–2 tablespoons cold water

FILLING
500 g peeled, seeded
pumpkin
¾ cup golden syrup
4 eggs, lightly beaten
½ cup cream
1 teaspoon cinnamon
¼ teaspoon ground nutmeg
whipped or clotted cream to serve

To make the pastry, sift the flour and icing sugar into a bowl. Rub the butter into the flour until the mixture resembles coarse breadcrumbs. Add the yolk and enough water to mix to a stiff dough. (Pastry can be made in a food processor.) Gather the dough into a ball, cover with plastic wrap and refrigerate for 30 minutes. To prepare the filling, chop the pumpkin into chunks. Boil or microwave until tender. Drain well, then mash. While the pumpkin is still hot, stir in the golden syrup. Mix well. Cool, then stir in the remaining ingredients. Roll the dough out on a lightly floured surface to fit a 24-cm-round, 3.5-cm-deep flan tin. Transfer the dough to tin and trim off any excess. Prick the base. Refrigerate the pastry base for 10 minutes, then freeze for 5 minutes. Bake blind at 190°C for 12 minutes. (To bake blind, cut a circle of baking paper to cover the pastry. Fill with dried beans or rice.) Remove the baking blind material and return to oven for 3–4 minutes to dry out the pastry base. Reduce the oven temperature to 180°C. Pour the filling into pastry case. Bake for 45 minutes until the filling has set. Serve warm with cream.
Serves 8.
N.B. The water content of butternut pumpkin is too high to use in this recipe.

CHELSEA BUNS

1 tablespoon sugar

½ cup tepid water

1 tablespoon Edmonds

active yeast

½ cup milk

50 g butter

2 eggs

4 cups Edmonds high grade flour

25 g butter

½ cup brown sugar

1 teaspoon mixed spice

½ cup sultanas

½ cup currants

Dissolve first measure of sugar in water. Sprinkle over yeast. Leave for 10 minutes or until frothy. Place milk in a small saucepan and heat until just before it boils. Add first measure of butter and stir until melted. Cool. Beat in eggs until combined. Place flour in a large bowl. Make a well in the centre. Pour in yeast and milk mixtures. Mix with a wooden spoon until combined. Turn onto a lightly floured surface and knead until smooth and elastic. Place dough in a greased bowl. Turn dough over. Cover with plastic wrap and set aside in a warm place until double in bulk. Punch dough down. Turn onto a floured surface and knead until smooth. Roll dough into a 35 cm square. Melt second measure of butter and use to brush dough liberally. Combine brown sugar, spice, sultanas and currants. Sprinkle over the dough and then roll up as for a Swiss roll. Cut into 2.5 cm slices. Place buns on a greased oven tray, close together but not touching. Cover with a clean cloth. Put in a warm place and leave to rise until buns are touching each other. Bake at 190°C for 30–35 minutes or until golden. Ice with White Icing (see page 112) or Pink Icing if wished.

Makes 12.

N.B. For Pink Icing, prepare White Icing and add 2 drops of red food colouring. Serve warm.

HONEY TEA BUNS

3 cups Edmonds standard flour
4 teaspoons Edmonds baking powder
½ teaspoon salt
1 teaspoon ground ginger
75 g butter
1 egg, beaten
2 tablespoons liquid honey
1 teaspoon grated orange rind
1 cup milk
extra milk to glaze
sugar to sprinkle
cinnamon to sprinkle

Sift flour, baking powder, salt and ginger into a bowl. Cut in butter until it resembles fine breadcrumbs. Add egg, honey and orange rind. Add sufficient milk to mix to a smooth, firm dough. On a lightly floured surface roll out dough to 2.5 cm thickness. Cut into rounds using a 5-cm-round biscuit cutter. Place on a greased oven tray. Brush tops with milk. Sprinkle with sugar and cinnamon. Bake at 200°C for 15 minutes or until pale golden.
Makes 15.

HOT CROSS BUNS

1½ cups milk

1 teaspoon sugar

2 tablespoons Edmonds active yeast

125 g butter, softened

¾ cup sugar

1 egg

¾ cup currants

½ cup sultanas

2 teaspoons mixed spice

1 teaspoon ground cinnamon

1 tablespoon mixed peel

6 cups Edmonds high grade flour

CROSSES

½ cup Edmonds standard flour

6 tablespoons water,
approximately

GLAZE

1 tablespoon sugar

1 tablespoon water

1 teaspoon gelatine

Heat milk and sugar until lukewarm. Add yeast and set aside until frothy. Cream butter and sugar until light and fluffy. Add egg, currants, sultanas, mixed spice, cinnamon and peel. Sift flour into a large bowl. Add yeast and fruit mixture alternately and combine to a firm but pliable dough using more flour if necessary. Turn out onto a floured surface and knead for 10 minutes. Place in a greased bowl and leave in a warm place to double in bulk. Punch down dough and shape ¼ cups of mixture into balls. Place side by side in two 20 x 30 cm greased sponge roll tins. Cover and leave to rise in a warm place until double in size. Pipe a cross on each bun. To make the crosses, mix flour and water to a smooth paste that is a suitable consistency for piping. Place mixture in a small plastic bag. Snip across one corner to form a hole. Twist top of bag. Bake at 200°C for 15–20 minutes or until golden. Remove from oven and brush with glaze. To make the glaze, place all ingredients in a small saucepan. Stir over a low heat until sugar and gelatine have dissolved. Cool hot cross buns on a wire rack.

Makes 18 buns.

BAGELS

2 teaspoons sugar

1½ cups tepid water

1 tablespoon Edmonds active yeast

4 cups Edmonds high grade flour

1 teaspoon salt

¼ cup sugar

1 egg

1 tablespoon water

Dissolve first measure of sugar in water. Sprinkle over yeast and leave for about 10 minutes or until frothy. Combine flour and salt in a bowl. Mix to combine. Pour in yeast mixture and mix until a stiff dough, adding more water if necessary. Knead dough until smooth and elastic. Place dough in a greased bowl. Turn dough over. Cover with plastic wrap and set aside in a warm place until double in bulk. Punch dough down. Form into a cylinder and break into 18 even-sized pieces. Roll each piece into a ball. Make a hole in the centre of the ball by pushing your finger through and spinning the dough around to make a large hole, the size of a small fist. Dust bagels with flour. Cover with a clean cloth. Set aside and leave to rise in a warm place for about 30 minutes. Dissolve second measure of sugar in a large saucepan of boiling water. Cook one bagel at a time in the boiling water for 30 seconds on each side. Remove with a slotted spoon. Drain and place on a greased baking tray. Brush well with egg glaze. To make the egg glaze, whisk together egg and water. Bake at 200°C for 15–20 minutes or until bagels sound hollow when tapped. Cool on a wire rack.
Makes 18.

CORNBREAD

1 cup Edmonds standard flour

1 teaspoon salt

2 tablespoons Edmonds baking powder

2 teaspoons chilli powder

1 cup fine polenta

2 eggs

300 g can cream-style corn

½ cup milk

1 cup grated tasty cheese

Sift flour, salt, baking powder and chilli powder into a bowl. Mix in polenta. Mix eggs, corn and milk together. Pour into dry ingredients and mix quickly until just combined. Pour mixture into a 24 x 13 cm loaf tin lined on the base with baking paper. Sprinkle with grated cheese and bake at 180°C for 45–60 minutes or until an inserted skewer comes out clean. Cool in tin for 10 minutes before turning out onto a wire rack.

BROWN BREAD
(NO-KNEAD BREAD)

1 cup kibbled wheat

1 cup boiling water

2 cups Edmonds wholemeal flour

2 teaspoon salt

2 tablespoons Edmonds
Surebake yeast

1 cup cold water

1 tablespoon golden syrup

1 cup boiling water

1 egg

3 cups Edmonds high grade flour

Combine kibbled wheat and boiling water. Set aside for 20 minutes. Combine wholemeal flour, salt, and yeast in a bowl. Add cold water and golden syrup, immediately followed by boiling water. Stir to a smooth paste. Mix in kibbled wheat. Stand for 2–3 minutes. Mix in egg and flour, adding the last cup of white flour slowly (more or less than the cup may be needed to give a very thick batter, which is not quite as stiff as a dough). Beat with an electric mixer on medium speed for 1–2 minutes or by hand for 3–4 minutes. Cover and put in a warm place for 15 minutes. Stir well and pour into two 22 cm x 13 cm greased loaf tins. Cover and stand in a warm place until the dough doubles in volume. Bake at 200°C for 35 minutes or until the loaf sounds hollow when tapped on base of bread. If loaf is browning too quickly cover with foil.

Makes 2 loaves.

Brown Bread (Top right)
White Bread (Bottom left)
Wholemeal Bread (Bottom right)

WHITE BREAD

5 cups Edmonds high grade flour

1 teaspoon sugar

1 teaspoon salt

2 tablespoons Edmonds
Surebake yeast

¾ cup cold water

2 tablespoons oil

¾ cup boiling water

oil

1 egg yolk

1 tablespoon water

sesame seeds, oat bran or poppy
seeds to sprinkle (optional)

Combine 2 cups of the flour, sugar, salt and yeast in a large bowl. Add cold water and oil, immediately followed by boiling water. Stir to a smooth paste and stand 2–3 minutes. Gradually mix 2 cups of flour into the yeast mixture. When flour is mixed in, turn out onto a lightly floured surface, using part of the reserved cup of flour for this. Knead dough until smooth and elastic. If the dough is still sticky, add a little of the remaining measured flour, kneading until smooth and elastic, or until dough springs back when lightly touched. Lightly brush large bowl with oil. Place dough in bowl. Brush top with a little oil. Cover. Put in a warm place until double in size. Punch dough down in the centre. Carefully take dough out of bowl and turn onto a lightly floured surface. Knead for 5 minutes. Divide dough in half. Shape each portion into a ball. Place the two balls side by side in a greased deep 22 cm x 13 cm loaf tin. Cover. Leave in a warm place until double in size or until dough reaches top of tin. Brush surface of dough with egg wash. To make the egg wash, whisk together yolk and water. If wished, sesame seeds, oat bran or poppy seeds can be sprinkled on top. Bake at 200°C for 30 minutes or until loaf sounds hollow when tapped on base of bread.

WHOLEMEAL BREAD

1¼ cups hot water

¼ cup honey

¾ cup milk

1 tablespoon Edmonds active yeast

4 cups Edmonds wholemeal flour

2 cups Edmonds high grade flour

1½ teaspoons salt

50 g butter

Combine hot water, honey and milk. Leave to cool until lukewarm. Sprinkle yeast over and leave for 10 minutes or until frothy. Combine 3 cups of the wholemeal flour, high grade flour and salt in a bowl. Set remaining cup of wholemeal flour aside. Cut in butter until it resembles coarse breadcrumbs. Make a well in the centre of the flour. Add frothy yeast mixture. Stir until well mixed. Turn out onto a lightly floured surface, using part of the reserved cup of flour for this. Knead the dough until smooth and elastic. If it is still sticky, add a little of the reserved flour, kneading until smooth or until dough springs back when lightly touched. Lightly oil a bowl.
Place dough in bowl and brush lightly with oil. Cover and leave in a warm place until double in size. Punch dough down in the centre, then lightly knead. Divide dough in half. Shape into ovals. Place dough into two greased 22 cm x 13 cm loaf tins. Cover and leave until dough rises to top of tins. Bake at 200°C for 40 minutes or until loaf sounds hollow when tapped on base of bread.

CHRISTMAS TREATS

RICH CHRISTMAS CAKE

¾ cup dark rum or brandy

1¾ cups orange juice

2 tablespoons grated orange zest

500 g currants

500 g raisins

400 g sultanas

2 cups chopped dates

150 g crystallised ginger, chopped

150 g packet mixed peel

150 g packet glacé cherries, halved

½ teaspoon vanilla essence

¼ teaspoon almond essence

2 teaspoons grated lemon zest

1 cup blanched almonds

2½ cups Edmonds high grade flour

½ teaspoon Edmonds baking soda

1 teaspoon cinnamon

1 teaspoon mixed spice

½ teaspoon ground nutmeg

250 g butter, softened

1½ cups brown sugar

2 tablespoons treacle

5 eggs

GLAZE and DECORATION

¼ cup apricot jam

1 teaspoon gelatine

1 tablespoon cold water

halved cherries, halved dried apricots

blanched almonds

In a saucepan, bring to boil rum, orange juice and zest. Remove from heat. Add dried fruit. Cover and leave overnight. Stir essences, lemon zest and almonds into saucepan. Sift flour, soda and spices into a bowl. In another bowl, cream butter, sugar and treacle until light and fluffy. Add eggs one at a time, beating well after each egg. Fold in sifted ingredients alternately with fruit mixture. Line a deep, square 23 cm tin with two layers of brown paper then one layer of baking paper. Spoon mixture into tin. Bake at 150°C for 4 hours or until an inserted skewer comes out clean when tested. Cover tin with a piece of brown paper for first 2 hours of cooking to prevent top from browning too quickly. Leave in tin until cold. To glaze and decorate: Make glaze by melting jam. Push through a fine sieve. Sprinkle gelatine over cold water. Sit over bowl of hot water and stir until gelatine dissolves. Stir into jam. Brush top of cake with half the glaze. Arrange dried fruit and nuts. Brush with remaining glaze. Allow to set before wrapping in foil. Store in a cool place.

FESTIVE CHOCOLATE RUM CAKE

125 g butter, softened

¾ cup caster sugar

2 eggs

1¾ cups Edmonds standard flour

½ cup cocoa

1 teaspoon Edmonds baking powder

1 teaspoon Edmonds baking soda

¾ cup warm milk

3 teaspoons instant coffee powder

¼ cup rum

GANACHE

150 g dark chocolate, chopped
(or melts or bits)

¼ cup cream

whipped cream and chocolate
shapes to garnish

icing sugar to dust

Cream butter and sugar until light and fluffy. Add eggs one at a time, beating well after each addition. Sift flour, cocoa and baking powder. Dissolve baking soda in milk, then whisk in coffee and rum. Fold dry ingredients and milk mixture alternately into butter mixture. Spoon into a greased 20 cm round cake tin that has been lined with baking paper on the base. Bake at 180°C for 45 minutes or until a skewer inserted in the centre of the cake comes out clean. Cool in tin for 10 minutes before transferring to a wire rack. When cold, cut cake horizontally into 3 equal portions. Place one portion on a serving plate and spread with half the ganache. Top with second portion and spread with remaining ganache. Place final portion of cake on top. To make the ganache, place chocolate and cream in a small saucepan. Stir over a low heat until chocolate melts and mixture is smooth. To serve, cut into wedges. Garnish with whipped cream and chocolate shapes. Dust with icing sugar.

CHOCOLATE SHAPES

Draw desired shapes onto baking paper. Pipe melted chocolate to outline. Randomly pipe lines inside shapes. Leave to set before removing from the paper.

BOILED FRUIT CAKE

500 g mixed fruit
water
250 g butter, chopped
1½ cups sugar
3 eggs, beaten

3 cups Edmonds standard flour
4 teaspoons Edmonds
baking powder
½ teaspoon almond essence
½ teaspoon vanilla essence

Put mixed fruit in a saucepan. Add just enough water to cover fruit. Cover and bring to the boil. Remove from heat. Stir in butter and sugar, stirring constantly until butter has melted. Allow to cool. Beat in eggs. Sift flour and baking powder into fruit mixture, stirring to combine. Stir in essences. Line a 24 cm round cake tin with two layers of brown paper followed by one layer of baking paper. Spoon mixture into cake tin. Bake at 160°C for 1½–2 hours or until an inserted skewer comes out clean. Leave in tin for 10 minutes before turning out onto a wire rack.

CATHEDRAL LOAF

125 g glacé pineapple rings

3 glacé pears

⅓ cup glacé green cherries

½ cup glacé red cherries

125 g glacé apricots

125 g blanched almonds

250 g whole brazil nuts

½ cup crystallised ginger

3 eggs

½ cup caster sugar

1 teaspoon vanilla essence

2 tablespoons brandy

¾ cup Edmonds standard flour

½ teaspoon Edmonds
baking powder

1 teaspoon ground nutmeg

¼ teaspoon salt

Chop pineapple rings and pears into 6 pieces. Halve green and red cherries. Chop apricots into quarters. Put chopped fruits, almonds, brazil nuts and ginger into a bowl. Mix to combine. In a separate bowl beat eggs, sugar, essence and brandy together. Sift flour, baking powder, nutmeg and salt together. Fold sifted ingredients into egg mixture. Pour onto fruit and nuts, mixing thoroughly. Line a 23 cm loaf tin with two layers of brown paper followed by one layer of baking paper. Pour mixture into loaf tin. Bake at 150°C for 2 hours or until an inserted skewer comes out clean. Allow to cool in tin. Remove paper and wrap in foil to store. Leave for 2 days before cutting. To serve, use a sharp knife to cut into thin slices.

CASSATA

1 litre chocolate ice cream
½ teaspoon vanilla essence
500 ml vanilla ice cream
½ cup toasted slivered almonds
½ cup chopped dark chocolate
1 cup chopped glacé fruit (e.g. papaya, apricots, pineapple)
melon balls to garnish (optional)

Soften chocolate ice cream and mix in essence. Use to line the base and sides of a 1 litre pudding basin. Freeze until firm. Soften vanilla ice cream. Fold in almonds, chocolate and glacé fruit. Use to fill the chocolate ice cream cavity. Cover with foil and freeze until firm. Unmould onto a serving plate by dipping bowl into hot water 2–3 times, then inverting onto a plate and shaking sharply. Cut into wedges to serve. Garnish with melon balls.
Serves 6–8.

CHOCOLATE ÉCLAIRS

100 g butter	**CHOCOLATE ICING**
1 cup water	2 cups icing sugar
1 cup Edmonds standard flour	2 tablespoons cocoa
3 eggs	¼ teaspoon butter
whipped cream	¼ teaspoon vanilla essence
	2 tablespoons boiling
	water, approx.

Combine butter and water in a saucepan. Bring to a rolling boil. Remove from heat and quickly add flour. Beat with a wooden spoon until mixture leaves the sides of the saucepan. Allow to cool for 5 minutes. Add eggs one at a time, beating well after each addition, until mixture is glossy. Pipe 7 cm strips of the mixture onto greased oven trays. Bake at 200°C for 30 minutes or until éclairs are puffy and golden, then lower heat to 120°C and continue baking for about 15 minutes until dry. Cool thoroughly. Using a sharp knife, cut slits into the sides of each éclair. Fill with whipped cream and ice tops with Chocolate Icing. To make the Chocolate Icing, sift icing sugar and cocoa into a bowl. Add butter and essence. Add sufficient boiling water to mix to a spreadable consistency.
Makes 30.

CREAM PUFFS

Pipe or spoon heaped teaspoons of Chocolate Éclair mixture onto greased oven trays. Bake as above. Cool thoroughly. Fill with whipped cream and strawberries. Dust with icing sugar.

Chocolate Liqueur Mousse (Top left)
Chocolate Log (Top right)
Chocolate Éclairs (Cream Puff variation) (Bottom)

CHOCOLATE LIQUEUR MOUSSE

200 g cooking chocolate

3 eggs

¼ cup sugar

1 tablespoon brandy, chocolate or coffee liqueur

300 ml cream, whipped

whipped cream to garnish

flaked or grated chocolate to garnish

Break chocolate into the top of a double boiler. Stir over hot water until chocolate has melted. Allow to cool slightly. Using an electric mixer, beat eggs and sugar for about 5 minutes, until thick and pale. Add chocolate and beat until just combined. Using a large metal spoon, fold in brandy and whipped cream. Pour into six individual dishes or one large dish. Chill until firm. Decorate with whipped cream and chocolate. Serves 6.

CHOCOLATE LOG

3 eggs

½ cup sugar

½ teaspoon vanilla essence

2 tablespoons cocoa

¼ cup Edmonds standard flour

1 teaspoon Edmonds
baking powder

25 g butter, melted

1 tablespoon water

icing sugar

raspberry jam

whipped cream

CHOCOLATE ICING
(see page 179)

Beat eggs, sugar and essence until thick and pale. Sift cocoa, flour and baking powder together. Fold into egg mixture then fold in butter and water. Pour mixture evenly over the base of a 20 x 30 cm sponge roll tin lined on the base with baking paper. Bake at 190°C for 10–12 minutes or until cake springs back when lightly touched. When cooked turn onto baking paper sprinkled with sifted icing sugar. Spread with jam and roll from the short side immediately, using the paper to help. Leave the roll wrapped in the paper until cold, then unroll, fill with whipped cream and re-roll gently. Ice with Chocolate Icing.

CHRISTMAS PUDDING

1 cup sultanas

1 cup raisins

1 cup currants

70 g packet blanched
almonds, chopped

150 g packet mixed peel

1 cup shredded suet

1 cup Edmonds standard flour

1½ teaspoons Edmonds
baking powder

1 teaspoon mixed spice

1 teaspoon cinnamon

¼ teaspoon ground nutmeg

¼ teaspoon salt

1½ cups soft breadcrumbs

1 cup brown sugar

2 eggs

2 teaspoons grated lemon zest

½ cup milk

1 tablespoon brandy

Put sultanas, raisins, currants, almonds and mixed peel into a large bowl. Add suet, mixing to combine. Sift flour, baking powder, mixed spice, cinnamon, nutmeg and salt into fruit mixture. Stir well. Add breadcrumbs and mix through. In a separate bowl, beat brown sugar, eggs, lemon zest and milk together. Add to fruit mixture, mixing thoroughly to combine. Stir in brandy. Spoon mixture into a well-greased 6-cup-capacity pudding basin. Cover with pleated greaseproof paper or foil. Secure with string, leaving a loop to lift out pudding when cooked. Place a trivet or old saucer in the bottom of a large saucepan half-filled with boiling water. Carefully lower pudding into saucepan making sure the water comes two-thirds of the way up the sides of basin. Cover and cook for 5 hours, making sure water is constantly bubbling. Check water level from time to time. Remove from saucepan. Leave until cold. Wrap well and store in refrigerator until ready to use. Steam for a further 2 hours before serving. Serve with Brandy Custard (see page 184).
Serves 6.

Christmas Pudding (Top right)
Brandy Custard (Left)

BRANDY CUSTARD

3 tablespoons Edmonds custard powder

2 tablespoons sugar

1½ cups milk

1 tablespoon butter

2 tablespoons brandy or rum

pinch of nutmeg

In a saucepan, mix custard powder, sugar and ¼ cup of the milk to a smooth paste. Add remaining milk. Stir over a low heat until mixture thickens and comes to the boil. Remove from heat. Stir in butter, brandy and nutmeg.
Makes 1½ cups.

ORANGE MARINATED STRAWBERRIES

¼ cup thinly pared orange zest
1 cup freshly squeezed orange juice
¼ cup sugar
1 large chip or 400 g strawberries

Cut orange zest into thin strips. Place orange zest, juice and sugar in a saucepan. Bring to the boil and simmer for 5 minutes. Leave to cool. Hull strawberries and cut in half. Place in a bowl. Pour over orange mixture. Leave to marinate for 2 hours at room temperature or overnight in the refrigerator, mixing regularly. Serve lightly chilled.

Serves 4.

FESTIVE TIRAMISU TERRINE

3 teaspoons instant coffee
¾ cup boiling water
¼ cup brandy
250 g packet sponge fingers
100 g dark chocolate, chopped
(or bits or melts)

300 ml cream
1 teaspoon gelatine
1 tablespoon cold water
¼ cup icing sugar
300 g mascarpone cheese
10–12 whole strawberries, hulled

Dissolve coffee in boiling water. Stir in brandy. Line a 21 cm x 11 cm loaf tin with plastic wrap so that it extends over the side of the tin. One by one, quickly dip 8 biscuits into the coffee mixture. Line the base of the tin with the biscuits. Keep remaining coffee mixture. Combine chocolate and ¼ cup of the cream in the top of a double boiler or heatproof bowl. Place over simmering water. Stir constantly until chocolate melts and the mixture is smooth. Remove from heat. Sprinkle gelatine over cold water. Place over a bowl of hot water and stir until gelatine dissolves. Stir into chocolate. Whip remaining cream and icing sugar together. Place mascarpone in a medium bowl. Beat with a wooden spoon until smooth. Fold in cream and chocolate. Spoon half the mixture evenly over biscuits. Place the strawberries in a line down the middle of the chocolate mixture. Carefully spoon over remaining chocolate mixture. Dip 9 more biscuits in reserved coffee mixture. Arrange on top of chocolate layer to cover completely. Fold plastic wrap over the terrine. Refrigerate for 4 hours. To serve, unfold plastic wrap from the top of the terrine. Invert onto a board or flat surface. Using a sharp knife, cut into slices.
Serves 6–8.

INDIVIDUAL BAKED ALASKAS

ICE CREAM
½ cup blanched almonds, toasted
and chopped
¼ cup raisins
¼ cup red cherries, chopped
2 tablespoons chopped
mixed peel
¼ cup dark rum
3 eggs, at room temperature

¼ cup caster sugar
300 ml cream, whipped

MERINGUE
3 egg whites, at room
temperature
½ cup caster sugar
½ teaspoon vanilla essence

To make the Ice Cream, combine almonds, dried fruit and rum in a bowl. Set aside for 30 minutes. Separate eggs. Using an electric mixer, beat egg yolks for 2–3 minutes. Gradually add caster sugar, beating until thick and pale. Fold in cream. Beat egg whites until stiff but not dry. Fold into yolk mixture. Lastly, fold in fruit mixture. Divide between six 1-cup capacity teacups. Cover and freeze for at least 4 hours. Working quickly, remove ice cream from cups by dipping them quickly into hot water, then inverting onto an oven tray. Cover and return to the freezer for 1 hour. To make the Meringue, beat egg whites to a soft foam. Gradually add caster sugar, beating continuously. Add essence and beat until meringue is thick and glossy. Cover ice cream moulds with the meringue, peaking it slightly – the ice cream must be completely covered with meringue or it will melt when baked. Return Alaskas to the freezer for 15 minutes. Bake at 250°C for about 2 minutes until the meringue peaks are golden. Serve immediately.

PAVLOVA

4 egg whites
1½ cups caster sugar
1 teaspoon white vinegar
1 teaspoon vanilla essence
1 tablespoon Edmonds Fielder's cornflour
whipped cream
fresh berries and mint leaves to garnish

Preheat oven to 180°C. Using an electric mixer, beat egg whites and caster sugar for 10–15 minutes or until thick and glossy. Mix vinegar, essence and cornflour together. Add to meringue. Beat on high speed for a further 5 minutes. Line an oven tray with baking paper. Draw a 22 cm circle on the baking paper. Spread the pavlova to within 2 cm of the edge of the circle, keeping the shape as round and even as possible. Smooth top surface. Place pavlova in preheated oven then turn oven temperature down to 100°C. Bake pavlova for 1 hour. Turn off oven. Open oven door slightly and leave pavlova in oven until cold. Carefully lift pavlova onto a serving plate. Decorate with whipped cream, fresh berries and mint leaves.
Serves 6.

SHERRY TRIFLE

4 tablespoons Edmonds custard powder

3 tablespoons sugar

2 cups milk

2 egg whites

200 g trifle sponge

¼ cup raspberry or apricot jam

¼ cup sherry

410 g can fruit salad

¾ cup cream

2 teaspoons icing sugar

¼ cup toasted slivered almonds to decorate

To make the custard, mix custard powder, sugar and ¼ cup of the milk to a smooth paste in a saucepan. Add remaining milk and stir over a low heat until mixture comes to the boil. Simmer for 2–3 minutes or until custard thickens, stirring constantly. Remove from heat, cover and leave until cold. When custard has cooled, beat egg whites until stiff. Fold custard into egg whites. Cut sponge in half horizontally. Spread cut surface with jam. Sandwich halves together. Cut into cubes then arrange in 6 individual serving dishes or 1 large serving bowl. Spoon sherry over sponge. Spoon fruit salad and juice evenly over sponge. Spoon custard over fruit salad. Chill until set. Beat cream and icing sugar until thick. Decorate trifles with cream and almonds.

N.B. To speed up the cooling of the custard, transfer mixture from the saucepan to a heatproof bowl. Stand in a bowl of iced water.

Serves 6.

SUMMER PUDDING

5 cups mixed berry fruit
1¼ cups sugar
10 slices stale toast-cut bread
8–10 fresh berries to garnish

Prepare fruit by washing, drying, hulling and slicing if large. Mix fruit and sugar together in a saucepan and heat gently until almost boiling. Remove from heat. Cool. Remove ¼ cup of berry juice and set aside. Cut crusts from bread and cut each slice into 3 fingers. Arrange bread around the inside of a 6-cup-capacity pudding basin. Spoon in one-third of the berry mixture. Layer with more bread and fruit. Repeat layers once more, finishing with a layer of bread. Spoon over enough berry juice to moisten bread. Cover with plastic wrap and weigh down with a heavy weight. Refrigerate for at least 2 hours or overnight. Turn onto a serving plate. Brush reserved juice over any sections of bread not soaked with juice. Garnish pudding with fresh berries.
Serves 6–8.

CHRISTMAS COOKIES

125 g butter, softened

¾ cup caster sugar

1 egg

1 teaspoon vanilla essence

2 cups Edmonds standard flour

½ teaspoon Edmonds baking powder

¼ cup cocoa

narrow ribbon to hang biscuits

Cream butter and sugar until light and fluffy. Add egg. Beat well. Beat in essence. Sift flour, baking powder and cocoa. Stir into creamed mixture, mixing to a soft dough. Shape dough into a ball. Cover with plastic wrap and refrigerate for 30 minutes. Roll dough out on a floured surface to a thickness of 5 mm. Using Christmas-shaped biscuit cutters, stamp out shapes. Place on greased oven trays. Using a metal or wooden skewer, make a small hole in the top of each biscuit. Bake at 180°C for 12 minutes. Cool on wire racks. To hang the biscuits from the Christmas tree, thread ribbon through the hole in the top of each biscuit, tying the ends together.

N.B. The biscuits will not stay fresh for longer than 1 day hanging from the tree.

Christmas Mince Pies (Top right)

Christmas Cookies (Left)

Christmas Mincemeat (Right)

CHRISTMAS MINCEMEAT

1¼ **cups currants**

1¼ **cups sultanas**

1¼ **cups raisins**

1¼ **cups mixed peel**

¼ **cup blanched almonds**

2 **medium apples, unpeeled, quartered and cored**

1 **cup brown sugar**

¼ **teaspoon salt**

½ **teaspoon ground nutmeg**

2 **tablespoons brandy or whisky or lemon juice**

Mince or finely chop currants, sultanas, raisins, peel and almonds. Finely chop or grate apples. Add apples, sugar, salt, nutmeg and brandy to fruit mixture. Mix well. Cover and refrigerate. Stir occasionally. Christmas Mincemeat will keep for up to 3 months in the refrigerator.

Makes 6 cups.

CHRISTMAS MINCE PIES

SWEET SHORTCRUST PASTRY
(or 400 g purchased sweet
shortcrust pastry)
1 cup Edmonds standard flour
75 g butter
¼ cup sugar

1 egg yolk
1 tablespoon cold water
1 cup Christmas Mincemeat
(see page 38)
1 egg, beaten
icing sugar to dust

To make the pastry, sift flour. Cut in butter until it resembles fine breadcrumbs. Stir in sugar. Add egg yolk and water. Mix to a stiff dough. Chill for 30 minutes before using. On a lightly floured board, roll out pastry to 3 mm thickness. Cut out rounds using a 7 cm cutter, and use to line about 16 patty tins. Using a 6 cm round biscuit cutter, cut out tops from the remaining pastry. Spoon teaspoons of Christmas Mincemeat into each base. Brush the edges of the bases with some of the egg. Place tops over the filling, pressing lightly around the edges to seal the pies. Glaze with the remaining beaten egg. Bake at 180°C for 15 minutes or until golden. To serve, heat at 140°C for 15 minutes or until warm. Dust with icing sugar.
Makes 16.

FLORENTINES

125 g butter, softened
½ cup sugar
5 tablespoons golden syrup
¼ cup Edmonds standard flour
70 g packet sliced almonds
½ cup chopped glacé cherries
½ cup chopped walnuts
¼ cup chopped mixed peel
150 g cooking chocolate, melted

Cream butter and sugar. Beat in syrup. Sift in flour. Add almonds, cherries, walnuts and peel. Mix well. Place level tablespoons of mixture on trays lined with baking paper, spacing them well apart to allow for spreading. Cook four at a time. Press each one out as flat and round as possible, using a knife. Bake in the oven at 180°C for 10 minutes or until golden brown. Remove from oven and leave on tray for 5 minutes before transferring to a wire rack. When cold spread melted chocolate on the flat side of each biscuit.
Makes 24.

Meringues (Top)
Florentines (Left)
Tiny Lemon Curd Tartlets (Right)

MERINGUES

2 egg whites
½ cup caster sugar
whipped cream

Using an electric mixer, beat egg whites until stiff but not dry. Add half the sugar and beat well. Repeat with remaining sugar. Pipe or spoon small amounts of meringue onto a greased oven tray. Bake at 120°C for 1–1½ hours or until the meringues are dry but not brown. Cool. Store unfilled meringues in an airtight container. To serve, sandwich together with whipped cream or serve as an accompaniment to fresh fruit salad and whipped cream.
Makes 18.

TINY LEMON CURD TARTLETS

LEMON CURD FILLING
1 tablespoon finely grated
lemon zest
¼ cup lemon juice
2 eggs, lightly beaten
50 g butter
¼ cup caster sugar

PASTRY
100 g butter, softened
¼ cup caster sugar
1 egg yolk
1 cup Edmonds standard flour

To make the Lemon Curd Filling, combine lemon zest and juice, eggs, butter and sugar in the top of a double boiler or in a heatproof bowl. Place over simmering water. Stir constantly until sugar dissolves and curd thickens. Remove from heat. Cover and cool.

For the Pastry, cream butter and sugar until light and fluffy. Add egg yolk and beat well. Stir in flour. Gather pastry into a ball and wrap in plastic wrap. Refrigerate for 20 minutes. Roll pastry out on a lightly floured surface to a thickness of 2–3 mm. Using a 7 cm round biscuit cutter, cut circles from pastry. Transfer to deep mini muffin tins. Prick bases with a fork. Freeze for 5 minutes. Bake at 180°C for 10 minutes until golden. Remove pastry cases from tins and cool on a wire rack. Just before serving, fill with lemon curd.

Makes 24 tartlets.

BRANDY BALLS

250 g packet Vanilla Wine biscuits
2 tablespoons currants
2 tablespoons chopped walnuts
1 egg
¼ cup sugar
1 tablespoon cocoa
1½ tablespoons brandy or sherry
125 g butter, melted
coconut or chocolate hail

Finely crush biscuits. Combine biscuit crumbs, currants and walnuts in a bowl. In another bowl lightly beat the egg with a fork. Add sugar and cocoa, stirring until thoroughly mixed. Add brandy. Pour into crumb mixture. Add melted butter. Stir until well combined. Measure level tablespoons of mixture and shape into balls. Roll in coconut or chocolate hail. Chill until firm.
Makes about 26.

RUM BALLS
Add 1½ tablespoons of rum in place of the brandy.

Chocolate Fudge (Top right)
Coconut Ice (Left)
Brandy Balls (Right)

CHOCOLATE FUDGE

2 cups sugar

2 tablespoons cocoa

½ cup milk

25 g butter

½ teaspoon vanilla essence

½ cup chopped walnuts (optional)

Put sugar and cocoa into a saucepan. Mix to combine. Add milk and butter. Heat gently, stirring constantly until sugar has dissolved and butter has melted. Bring to the boil. Do not stir. Let mixture boil until the soft ball stage. To test for soft ball stage, drop a small amount of mixture off a teaspoon into cold water. When a soft ball forms, the mixture is ready. On a sugar thermometer, the soft ball stage is 116°C. Remove from heat. Add essence and leave to stand for 5 minutes. Stir in walnuts. Beat with a wooden spoon until thick. Pour into a buttered tin. Mark into squares. Cut when cold.

COCONUT ICE

4 cups icing sugar
½ cup milk
2 tablespoons butter
¼ teaspoon salt

1 cup coconut
few drops of red food
colouring (optional)

Put icing sugar, milk, butter and salt into a saucepan. Heat gently, stirring constantly until sugar dissolves. Bring to the boil. Do not stir. Let mixture boil until the soft ball stage. To test for soft ball stage, drop a small amount of mixture off a teaspoon into cold water. When a soft ball forms, the mixture is ready. On a sugar thermometer, the soft ball stage is 116°C. Add coconut. Remove from heat and allow to cool for 10 minutes. Beat until mixture starts to thicken. Pour into a buttered tin. Allow to cool. Cut into squares.

N.B. If desired, divide the mixture in half before beating and add a few drops of red food colouring to one portion. Beat the white portion until it starts to thicken. Spread this mixture on top of pink mixture.

YULETIDE CARAMELS

2½ cups sugar	25 g butter
2 tablespoons coconut	½ cup milk
1 teaspoon ground ginger	1 teaspoon vanilla essence
1 tablespoon golden syrup	

Put sugar, coconut and ginger into a saucepan. Mix to combine. Add golden syrup, butter and milk. Heat gently, stirring constantly until sugar dissolves. Bring to the boil. Do not stir. Boil mixture until soft ball stage. To test for soft ball stage, drop a small amount of mixture off a teaspoon into cold water. When a soft ball forms, the mixture is ready. On a sugar thermometer, this is 116°C. Remove from heat. Add essence and beat until thick and creamy. Pour into a buttered tin. Mark into squares. Cut when cold.

RUSSIAN FUDGE

3 cups sugar	125 g butter
½ cup milk	⅛ teaspoon salt
½ cup sweetened condensed milk	1 tablespoon golden syrup

Put sugar and milk into a saucepan. Heat gently, stirring constantly until sugar dissolves. Add condensed milk, butter, salt and golden syrup. Stir until butter has melted. Bring to the boil and continue boiling to the soft ball stage, stirring occasionally to prevent burning. To test for soft ball stage, drop a small amount of mixture off a teaspoon into cold water. When a soft ball forms, the mixture is ready. On a sugar thermometer, the soft ball stage is 116°C. Remove from heat. Cool slightly. Beat until thick. Pour into a buttered tin. Mark into squares. Cut when cold.

N.B. Vanilla essence or chopped nuts may be added to fudge before beating.

Stained Glass Window Log (Top), Yuletide Caramels (Second from top), Hazelnut Chocolate Truffles (Third from top), Russian Fudge (Bottom)

STAINED GLASS WINDOW LOG

¾ cup brazil nuts, toasted and roughly chopped
10 red glacé cherries, halved
10 green glacé cherries, halved
12 dried apricots, quartered
250 g dark chocolate, roughly chopped (or melts or bits)
½ cup sweetened condensed milk
3 tablespoons cream

Combine nuts and dried fruit in a bowl. Place chocolate, condensed milk and cream in the top of a double boiler or heatproof bowl. Place over simmering water and stir constantly until chocolate melts and mixture is smooth. Remove from heat. Add nut and fruit mixture. Mix well. Lay a 45 cm length of foil on a flat surface. Transfer chocolate mixture to the centre of the foil. Fold the foil over the mixture, then roll into a log about 35 cm long. Twist the ends of the foil to enclose the log. Refrigerate for 3–4 hours until firm. To serve, cut into slices. Store in the refrigerator.

HAZELNUT CHOCOLATE TRUFFLES

250 g dark chocolate, chopped (or melts or bits)

25 g butter, chopped

½ cup cream

1 tablespoon Frangelico liqueur (optional)

¼ cup ground roasted hazelnuts

200 g dark chocolate, chopped (or melts or bits)

21 hazelnuts, halved, to garnish

Place chocolate and butter in the top of a double boiler or heatproof bowl. Place over simmering water. Stir constantly until chocolate melts and the mixture is smooth. Remove from heat. Stir in cream, liqueur and ground hazelnuts. Cover and refrigerate for several hours until firm. Roll teaspoons of mixture into balls. Place in a single layer on a plate. Cover with plastic wrap and refrigerate for 1 hour. To coat truffles, melt second measure of chocolate as above. Cool slightly. Quickly dip truffles into the melted chocolate using a dipping stick or teaspoons. Allow excess chocolate to drain off. Place on a sheet of foil. Garnish each truffle with half a hazelnut. Allow to dry before storing in a covered container in a cool place.
Makes 42 truffles.

DRIED FRUIT COMPOTE

2 cups freshly squeezed orange juice (about 8 oranges)

½ cup water

⅓ cup runny honey

2 cinnamon sticks

⅓ cup brandy

200 g dried apricots

150 g dried figs

100 g pitted prunes

Strain orange juice through a fine sieve into a saucepan. Add water, honey and one cinnamon stick. Stir over a low heat until honey dissolves. Bring to the boil, reduce heat and simmer for 45 minutes. Remove cinnamon stick and discard. Stir in brandy. Pack dried fruit and remaining cinnamon stick into a clean sterilised jar. Pour syrup over fruit. Cover jar tightly with a lid. Cool. Store in the refrigerator. Serve with whipped cream, ice cream or yoghurt.

PANETTONE

1 teaspoon sugar	½ teaspoon salt
¼ cup warm water	4 egg yolks, lightly beaten
4 teaspoons Edmonds active yeast	¾ cup sultanas
¾ cup milk	¼ cup mixed peel
75 g butter	finely grated zest of 1 lemon
4 cups Edmonds high grade flour	milk to brush
⅓ cup sugar	

Dissolve first measure of sugar in warm water. Sprinkle yeast over water. Set aside in a warm place for 10 minutes until frothy. Place milk and butter in a small saucepan. Stir over a low heat until butter melts. Transfer to a large bowl and allow to cool to lukewarm. Stir in frothy yeast mixture. Using a wooden spoon beat in 1 cup of the flour, and the sugar and salt. Cover with plastic wrap and stand in a warm place until mixture is bubbly. Mix yolks and remaining flour into the yeast mixture. Add sultanas, mixed peel and lemon zest. Mix to a soft dough with a wooden spoon. Turn dough onto a floured surface and knead for 10 minutes until smooth and elastic. Place dough in a lightly oiled bowl, turning to coat with oil. Cover with plastic wrap. Stand in a warm place until doubled in bulk (about 1½ hours). Punch dough down with a fist, then knead for 1 minute on a lightly floured surface. Form into a large ball and place in a greased, deep, 20 cm round cake tin that has been lined with baking paper on the base. Cover with plastic wrap and stand in a warm place until doubled in bulk. Brush top of Panettone with milk. Bake in the lower third of the oven at 200°C for 15 minutes, then reduce heat to 180°C and bake for a further 30 minutes or until bread sounds hollow when tapped. Leave in tin for 10 minutes before transferring to a wire rack to cool. To serve, cut into wedges. Serve buttered.

N.B. Panettone is best eaten on the day it is made, however it will keep for up to 4 days. It is delicious toasted.

STOLLEN

1 teaspoon sugar

¼ cup tepid water

1 tablespoon Edmonds active yeast

¾ cup milk

¼ cup sugar

100 g butter

½ teaspoon salt

3½ cups Edmonds high grade flour

1 egg

2 cups mixed dried fruit

½ cup toasted almonds

¼ cup brandy

200 g marzipan

melted butter

icing sugar to dust

Dissolve first measure of sugar in water. Sprinkle over yeast. Set aside until frothy. Heat milk, second measure of sugar, butter and salt together. Cool. Add yeast to milk mixture. Beat 1 cup of the flour into milk mixture with a wooden spoon. Cover and set aside in a warm place until batter is bubbly. Beat egg and mix into batter with remaining flour. Mix dried fruit, almonds and brandy together. Mix into dough. Turn onto a lightly floured board and knead until smooth and elastic. Place in a greased bowl. Turn dough over and cover with plastic wrap. Set aside in a warm place until double in bulk. Punch dough down and knead lightly. Shape dough into a 20 x 30 cm rectangle on a greased oven tray. Roll marzipan into a 30 cm roll. Place marzipan one-third of the way from the dough's long edge. Fold the remaining two-thirds of the rectangle over the marzipan to within 5 cm of the long edge. Brush with melted butter. Cover with a clean cloth. Set aside in a warm place until double in bulk. If preferred, cut the mixture in half and make two smaller Stollen. Bake at 200°C for 15 minutes. Reduce heat to 180°C and cook for 15 minutes or until Stollen sounds hollow when tapped. Cool and dust with icing sugar.

Stollen (Top left)

Panforte (Top right)

Almond Shortbread Rings (Left)

ALMOND SHORTBREAD RINGS

250 g butter, softened
1 cup icing sugar
3–4 drops almond essence
1½ cups Edmonds standard flour
¾ cup Edmonds Fielder's cornflour
70 g packet ground almonds

Cream butter and icing sugar until light and fluffy. Add essence. Sift flour and cornflour. Stir into butter mixture, along with ground almonds, mixing to a soft dough. Transfer dough to a lightly floured surface. Knead lightly for 2 minutes. Divide dough in half. Shape each portion into a ball and place in the centre of lightly greased oven trays. Pat or roll into a 20 cm round circle. Using a sharp knife or pizza wheel, divide dough into 8 equal portions, cutting almost right through the dough. Prick each section several times with a fork. Bake at 150°C for 40 minutes. Cool on a wire rack. To divide shortbread, break into sections along the marked lines.

INDEX